A Cradle in the Waves

A Cradle in the Waves

Anne-Marie Heckt

SwiftSong Press

Cover illustration, cover and interior design, map illustrations by Nina Noble Design
www.ninanobledesign.com

Sketches of Ferry House (Whidbey Island) and Castle House (Fort Worden) by A.M. Heckt

ISBN: 9780692642580

Library of Congress control number: 2016933509

Printed by Village Books
Bellingham, Washington

SwiftSong Press

*This book would not exist without Fort Worden,
the beauty of my home state, and the support
of my family. For my three wonderful men:
Steve, Gabriel, and Justin.
All the best things happened because of you.
All my love, always.*

AREA MAPS

To Strawberry Island
(Protection Island)

To Discovery Bay

Woods

Real stores on Water Street in 1862:

Waterman and Katz
Kentucky Store (Mr. Rothschild)
E.S. Fowler Wharf and Merchant
    "26 feet of water at low tide"
News Depot
Bakery
Livery, stable, horses
Washington Hotel

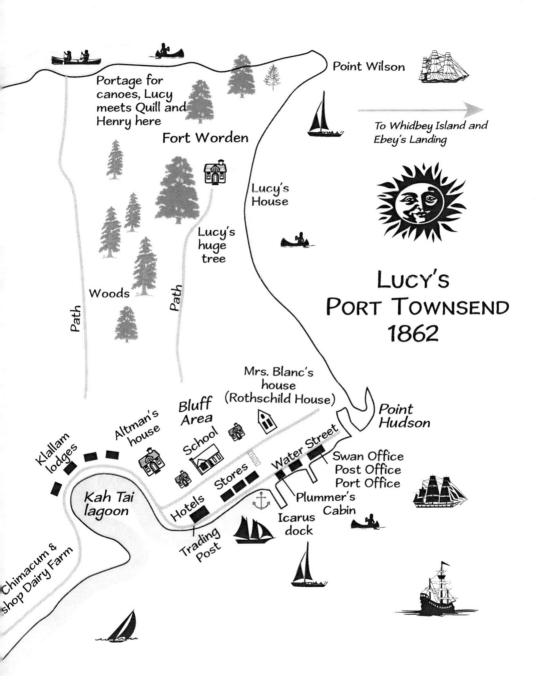

Portage for canoes, Lucy meets Quill and Henry here

Fort Worden

Point Wilson

To Whidbey Island and Ebey's Landing

Lucy's House

Lucy's huge tree

LUCY'S PORT TOWNSEND 1862

Woods

Path

Path

Mrs. Blanc's house (Rothschild House)

Point Hudson

Klallam lodges

Altman's house

Bluff Area

School

Stores

Water Street

Swan Office
Post Office
Port Office

Plummer's Cabin

Kah Tai lagoon

Hotels

Icarus dock

Trading Post

Chimacum & ...shop Dairy Farm

Lucy's Map of Port Townsend Vicinity

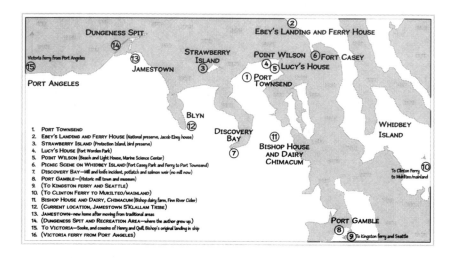

AUTHOR'S NOTE

A Cradle in the Waves was born when I stood on a cliff in the Pacific Northwest, wondering about the people who'd been there before me—the soldiers and families, and those passing by in canoes or sailing ships. I thought about how I'd visited as different versions of myself: a teen going to a dance workshop, a college student exploring the fields and bunkers, and a mother raising small children.

The book is fiction, but includes real people and events. It can be difficult to accept ourselves at different stages, much less people living over 150 years ago. Every effort has been made to be true to the people and place. Attitudes toward local Indians were often dismissive and disrespectful in 1862, and some of that language has been included to show a reality of that time.

Contents

August, 1862
Port Townsend
Washington Territory

Lucy clung to the edge of the dock and peered into the darkness of the waterfront. The row of buildings beyond the empty dock stood like silent sentries, their windows unlit. But she knew the town was not empty. Somewhere out there, a criminal and a young Klallam played cat and mouse—though which was the cat and which the mouse, she did not know.

Trying not to rock the boat, she strained to catch a glimpse of the boy who'd leapt out of the canoe minutes before. "Henry?" she called out in a whisper she hoped would carry, but there was no answer. She caught the echo of a faint sound: footsteps! Her hopes rose when a figure appeared in the alleyway, but it was only Henry's cousin looking for him.

Smoke hung in the air from the fire that raged nearby, and Lucy knew things would never be the same. From out in the bay she had seen the settlers defending their end of town, but they didn't seem to be doing anything for the Indian homes ablaze next to them. They had abandoned Henry's village to the flames. Lucy touched the arm of the girl in the canoe with her, but got no response. Quill's home was turning to ash nearby and her brother was out there with a dangerous man. Her glazed eyes probed the pools of shadow under the buildings at the quiet end of town.

Lucy hated waiting, and was about to climb onto the dock. Just then a shot rang out, glass shattered, and they heard a shout. Someone was running up the street toward them.

CHAPTER 1

The Wrong Clothes

Lucy studied Port Townsend from an island across the water. A cliff covered with dark trees towered over the buildings that huddled on the beach below. A cluster of Indian homes marked one end of town and the docks stuck out in the middle, like whiskers on an unshaved face. The *Icarus* floated there, its bright blues and yellows flashing against the dull background of brown and muddy green. It was hard to believe she'd left the *Icarus* only yesterday. When Lucy closed her eyes, she could still feel the rolling motion and felt a little queasy.

Her father had wakened her at first light to row over to the island with the school. "A picnic!" he told her, "to celebrate your arrival!" Like all teachers, he was convinced that open air and kites always spelled a happy day. Clearly, he had no idea how fast the weather could turn nasty here, nor could he possibly know how quick a pack of girls could do the same.

"Hey! Stuck up! Teacher's daughter!" taunted a voice behind Lucy.

Ignore a bully and they'll go away, she told herself, refusing to turn around. She looked down and realized she'd gotten too near the edge of the bluff while studying the town. Before she could step away, a hand planted itself between her shoulder blades and pushed. Lucy cried out and lurched toward the edge. She spun around, grabbing for something to stop her fall. The only thing she could reach turned out to be the meanest girl this side of the Continental Divide: Katherine Altman.

Katherine gave a rough shake. Lucy let go, noticing the ring of girls that had drawn up behind her. The cliff's edge made the back of Lucy's neck prickle. She inched her feet forward, but that put her closer to Katherine's bad breath. Her father had promised a fun day. "Fun?" she muttered, straightening her dress and glancing at the faces around her. *If this is fun, I wonder what funerals are like in these parts?*

"What did you say, little Miss Know-it-all?" Freckles and dirt stood out Katherine's nose. She had a chipped tooth, a ripped pocket, and a big toe sticking out of one boot.

As they waited for Lucy's reply, the girls' eyes drilled into her and she realized she was dressed all wrong. When her father told her she'd be attending a celebration, she'd put on her best dress. Everyone else wore homespun over the top of sturdy shoes. Their stares lingered on Lucy's puffed sleeves and then traveled down to her shiny white boots, like old ladies working on a corn cob. "Ting!" she wanted to say, every time they started over, "Ting! Ting! Ting!" like that new invention she'd viewed in San Francisco—what was it called?—the *typewriter*.

Katherine's heavy boot ground on top of Lucy's white one. Her toes smarted and the wind pierced her dress and stung her eyes until they watered. She tried to wipe them away without anyone noticing.

"She's crying!" Katherine crowed, delighted. "Cry baby!"

This always happened to Lucy when she got angry, curse her luck. Her skin turned all blotchy and her eyes started to leak. Not the *I'm so sad my flower died* kind of tears, but the *there's so much pressure in my head and I hate this girl so much I think I'll explode soon* kind of tears that came when her words were all choked up with a cork in them.

The perfect set-down would come later, while Lucy was feeding the chickens or cutting biscuits, one that would squelch Katherine and make all the other girls like her. But all she could do on the spot was smile weakly and wish she could get back on the *Icarus*.

She would sail through the Straits, past Vancouver's Island and out into the Pacific Ocean, then down the West Coast, eating moldy ship's biscuit and drinking muddy water. Even fighting through the waves and terror of the Cape would be worth the trouble. Because, if you were patient, the waters of the West eventually turned the corner into the friendly waters of the Atlantic, and so on to Boston... and home.

CHAPTER 2

The Wrong Path

Lucy woke into a silence that broke like a china teacup when she plunked her feet down on the cold pine floor. There was no sound of her mother's skirts swishing over the floorboards. There would be no flour drifting like dust motes in the early light, and no breakfast. She frowned. It wasn't like her mother to sleep so late.

Fog swirled outside the window.

"A little sun," she whispered into the silence. "Just a little, please?" But she pulled on her gray wool dress over her shift anyway. She wouldn't make the same mistake as at the picnic. Imagine, wool in May! So far as she'd seen it, the weather here could only come up with one color and that was gray: gray wind, gray skies, gray rain—sheets of it. She reached for her thickest stockings and then picked up her everyday boots, and sighed.

Lucy thought back over the last week of unpacking, scrubbing, digging, more scrubbing, and her first meeting with those horrible girls. She considered the meaning of the word "fun." Fun was drinking tea with her best friend Emily in her postage stamp-sized garden back in Boston, or spying on the older boys when they came for lessons with her father. Nowhere by any stretch of her imagination could she find a way to connect the word "fun" with Port Townsend.

She shook herself and tiptoed downstairs, avoiding the step that creaked. She glanced toward her parents' bedroom in the back and wondered if she should tell them she was stepping outside. *No,* she thought, *why bother them?* She opened the front door, thankful that the latch lifted soundlessly. Her father had just oiled it, as her mother had been needing so much more sleep lately. Lucy thought she was probably worn out from all the work involved in setting up house; but it was a little odd.

From the porch, all Lucy could see was trees and more dripping wet trees. "I hate it here," she said. No answer returned to her from the swirling fog.

She couldn't help thinking of Boston in May, with skies blue as a robin's egg and sun streaming in the windows. She'd pull on any old dress and step out the front door to see what her friends had planned for the day. Here, the sky felt like it was pressing down on her shoulders. Even on a Saturday, there was nothing to do and no one to do it with.

Something rustled in the bushes and Lucy froze. When a tiny rabbit hopped into view, she snorted. The boys had warned Lucy of wild things in the woods: bears, cougars, and huge birds that carried children off in their claws. She knew a tall tale when she heard one, but she hadn't been completely sure.

The rabbit twitched its whiskers and sniffed the air. She stood very still, hoping to get close enough to touch its velvet fur. A rabbit couldn't talk, but Lucy thought it might be the best she could do right now for company. As her mother always said, "When you're scraping the bottom of the barrel, you'd best learn to like what's down there."

She crept down the front porch steps. When she reached out the rabbit looked at her with large eyes, trembling. Then it sprang up and bounced away through the field. Lucy scrambled after it, dragging her skirts through the wet grass. When it finally stopped for a nibble, she scooped it up. She was able to hold onto the trembling body for an instant, but then it twisted and scratched until she had to let go. She watched the white tail disappear into the woods.

"Ouch! Even the animals hate strangers here!" Lucy said, rubbing the welts on her arms.

She leaned back to see the tops of trees she'd been told not to enter alone, ever. "This land's not yet civilized!" She'd heard it a thousand times already. But Lucy was in the habit of rescuing sick and wounded animals. She couldn't see the mother, and the thought of some beast snatching up the little thing made her stomach twist into a knot. She dived in, following a path that snaked through the trees. *Probably for deer,* Lucy told herself, not wanting to think what else might have been there, or who.

In the dim light, Lucy didn't see the gnarled tree root. She stumbled, ripping holes through all three pairs of stockings she'd put on to try and keep out the cold. Her mother would be furious! On the other hand, Lucy could point out that she'd grown up in Boston, where there were sidewalks, and she had no way of knowing a root could be as big as her leg. She scrambled to her feet and darted around another bend.

The rabbit sat in the middle of the path looking very satisfied with itself. Lucy stopped. Her heart pounded as she puffed out clouds of steam into the still air. A twig snapped nearby and the rabbit jumped again. A scurry through underbrush and brambles left Lucy even more mussed, and a little panicked. The path had disappeared, and so had the rabbit.

She tried to get her bearings. Thick trunks closed in around her like bars in a jail cell, and the light was dim. The weight of her dew-soaked dress pulled down on her, and blood trickled down her shin from her scuffed knee. She wondered if her parents were awake yet.

The fight she'd had with her father after the picnic played through her mind, again.

On their way home from the picnic, Lucy had planted herself in the middle of Port Townsend's muddy street and refused to move. Most of the shop owners stood in their doorways staring at them.

"Father, I want to go home," she'd said, remembering the feel of Katherine's hand in the middle of her back. The *Icarus* bobbed at the dock nearby, and one of the sailors waved at her from its deck. Lucy had almost lifted her white handkerchief, like a flag: *I surrender! Take me back!* But she knew her father would not find that amusing.

"Lower your voice, please," her father had said, directing a smile at the grocer. The thought had crossed Lucy's mind that a teacher who couldn't control his own daughter would be viewed poorly in a town like this, or any town for that matter.

"I could live with grandma and study at the French school. I could help with the younger students to earn my fees," she'd said. "I could be certified in a few years, and teach them myself for that matter!" She'd planted her hands on her hips, trying to look older than thirteen-going-on-fourteen. "I won't learn a thing here, at a primary school!"

"And you don't need to, Lucy." Her father had blown his breath out, ending in a sigh. "We both know that."

Taking her elbow, he'd steered her down the street. His voice had softened as he left the shop keepers behind. "It's only your second day!" He'd ruffled her hair, as though they were discussing ribbons or math facts. "This is your new home. Give it a chance to welcome you."

Lucy considered the meanings of words as she limped through the trees. *Fun, lucky, welcome...* She might as well throw away her copy of Mr. Webster's *New and Compleat Dictionary*. Though she loved the feel of its leather cover, worn soft with use, the definitions were all wrong for here—like all the clothes she'd packed in her trunk.

Up ahead, the shadows lightened between the trees. As a person of less-exalted stature (small, some would call her) and double cursed in being a teacher's daughter, Lucy knew that you had to act confident and move forward. No use going back, as she had no idea where back was. She sped up as the light grew stronger.

Finally, an opening! She rushed forward, and found herself with nothing more than air beneath her boot.

Rocks rattled down the side of the cliff. Lucy clung to the bush that had stopped her plunge, but it was pulling out of the ground. She took a breath, then a deeper one, trying to calm herself. The ground beneath her dropped, and her body jolted lower as part of the cliff crumbled.

The sand continued to slide away and Lucy's feet churned through the soil. Letting go for an instant to grasp a tree root, she teetered at the edge and then hauled herself up onto firm ground as the whole section she'd been on broke and gave way. She rolled back and then back even more, to be certain she'd reached solid ground. Then she lay still, gulping in air.

One boot had slipped off in the struggle and teetered on the new cliff edge. She groaned, but didn't dare move closer. The toe tipped forward as if stepping out for a walk. It bounced a few times, launched out into the air, and splashed into the water below.

As she watched the spinning boot, she wondered what she'd done to deserve yet another cliff edge in so few hours. Was it fate? She hadn't requested this particular part of the country. She hadn't asked for boys with tall tales and runny noses, or the cold weather. She positively had *not* asked for the likes of Katherine Altman.

She watched her shoe bob out into the waves. "Good luck!" she muttered, wondering where it would wind up. China? Mexico? Maybe even Boston? She imagined her boot floating up to the dock she'd left from months ago.

Lucy had wrenched her leg and her arms trembled. She'd never tell the boys, or those horrid girls, that she was afraid of the shadows under the trees and the rustling sounds in the brambles. Should she wait for someone to find her? Like in *Hansel and Gretel*, she wouldn't be surprised if this forest hid a witch with bad eyesight.

Bread crumbs! Lucy had an idea. She stood and shucked off her stockings; ripped them up and used the pieces, spearing them on thorns and twigs. After much work, she had marked off all the paths that led to the edges of the cliff with the fabric as warning flags. Hopefully the local birds didn't have a taste for stockings.

Lucy's mind skidded sideways every time she thought of facing her mother with the loss of both boot and stockings. Port Townsend was a fine spot if you were a logger, miner or trapper, but it was sorely lacking in proper shops. Easy to find a bit of tallow or tinned meat, but the clothing that made it round from the East Coast, or up from San Francisco, cost a pretty penny. Lucy had just badly stained her second dress. Until they got some washing done, she could choose between stiff-with-salt and stained-with-dirt. Or she could appear in her petticoat.

A chime went off in Lucy's mind like a repeating clock. How much time had passed?

She found a wider trail. Was it the original path? "A little luck, please!" she whispered.

The rabbit jumped out, right at her feet. She thought he looked very pleased with himself. "Look what you've done!" she said. "Where are we?" The rabbit turned and hopped along, and Lucy decided to follow it for luck. If one old rabbit's foot was lucky, surely all four was plenty?

She approached another clearing in the trees and slowed. She broke out into a large meadow and gave a sigh of relief. Grasses and flowers rolled away from her in gold, yellow and red, all baking in the morning light. Butterflies fluttered over wild sweet peas, and bees buzzed in the clover. The fog had melted away from the land, though a bank of it still covered the water. She could hear the lap of waves nearby.

She was beginning to relax when she spied something moving at the edge of the meadow—a bunch of somethings. She threw herself flat on the ground behind a rock.

CHAPTER 3

A Beginning

Lucy crawled forward to peek out through the cover of some reeds. A line of men with canoes on their shoulders marched along the meadow's edge, followed by a few old women and giggling girls. A shiver tickled Lucy's spine. Indians! She hadn't seen a whole group before. Just a few dark faces, quietly mixing with the bustle of the town. She remembered the EXTRA!'s she and her friends had read when parents weren't looking: stories about killings, burned cabins, and children left orphaned... or worse. She kept as still as possible while the sun beat down on her back and the sweat trickled between her shoulder blades.

After the last person disappeared over the hill, her rabbit popped out, bold as you please. Lucy considered for a moment and then stepped into the path. The rabbit hadn't noticed her, yet. The chime went off in her mind again.

Mother probably has half the town out looking for me by now.
On the other hand, they'd been asleep when she left.
But that was a long time ago.

She'd try one last time to catch the rabbit, and then hurry home. Lucy stretched out her fingers to reach a little farther. She lost her balance and tipped over as the rabbit leapt and two new faces came up over the hill. The first, a girl, darted forward and caught the animal by the scruff of the neck. The other, a boy, studied Lucy where she lay sprawled in the middle of their path. He frowned at her.

Standing and dusting off her dress, Lucy studied them back. The girl had a round face and dimples. She wore a simple gingham dress and her black hair was pleated in two neat braids with leather strips on the ends. She smiled at Lucy. The boy had a shock of thick black hair and his legs and arms stuck out of his clothing, like he'd had a recent bout of growing. He wore breeches with suspenders and an old hat tipped back on his head.

Their feet were bare, and Lucy caught the scents that mingled around them—of sea and pine, smoke, and a little bit of mystery. The sea smell reminded her of being on the ship those long weeks, with the salty air and tossing waves.

She felt an ache when she saw the girl cradle the rabbit like Lucy used to hold her tabby cat, with the feet sticking up. Her feelings must have shown on her face, because the girl held out the rabbit for Lucy. But it wiggled free, and the girls raced around in circles until the boy darted in and grabbed the animal by the scruff of the neck. He glared at both of them.

The rabbit dangled from the boy's hand. Lucy knew most boys out here would skin an animal soon as look at it. But just as he was about to break the little thing's neck, the girl stepped in, pulled a basket from her back and plopped the rabbit inside. She pushed down the lid and held it out to Lucy.

They were twins. Lucy could see it now. Faces like two halves of the same apple, with identical foreheads. But where the girl's face was full of laughter, the boy's was more guarded. He watched the basket as the girl pushed it into Lucy's arms.

"Thank you!" said Lucy.

"You are welcome," said the girl, patting the top.

"Oh!" Lucy startled. She hadn't thought the Indians spoke much English.

Voices called from the water and the boy strode off without another look, but the girl nodded her head at the basket. "Be careful," she said, and motioned holding the lid on tight. Then she left too.

Lucy's curiosity drew her up over the hill. The girl was climbing into the last canoe, and an old woman scolded—the clicks of her tongue echoing across the water as the boat bobbed and the boy waded through the waves to push off. The girl gave a half-wave in Lucy's direction and Lucy lifted her hand in return. Before jumping into the canoe, her twin turned to look back, still glaring. A bank of thick fog started at the edge of the water, and the canoe parted its white curtain and slipped out of sight.

As she stepped out of the woods with the basket, Lucy felt as if another cliff-edge loomed in front of her. Her mother was pacing back and forth on the porch. As Lucy drew near, she could see that her blonde hair had been hastily done, and her dress was askew. Lucy stiffened her spine and marched up the steps. The shaking her mother gave her rattled Lucy's teeth.

"Do you have any idea of the dangers out there?" Her mother asked.

The butterflies and the Indian girl's smiling face came to mind, but Lucy knew better than to answer back. She stood still while her mother's eyes took stock of her dirty dress, missing tights, and the bootless foot (which Lucy was trying to hide behind her other leg). When her eyes rested on the basket, her mother frowned and said, "What is that?" But then she shook her head as if to clear it and said, "We'll deal with that later. Put it away." By now, most of her hair had fallen from its pins and lay in a pile on her shoulders. She looked more tired than angry, and Lucy felt the stirrings of guilt somewhere near her empty stomach.

"But mother… "

"Do as I say."

A rabbit would definitely not be welcome inside the house. "But it's a… "

"Lucy!"

"Yes ma'am."

She carried the basket up to her room and peered in. The rabbit looked up at her with huge eyes and blinked. "You remind me of a boy who raced up and down our street back home," she told him. "I think I'll call you Dodger."

"Lucy!" her mother called.

"Coming!" she answered, hurrying to join her on the porch. "Where's father?"

Her mother's mouth flattened into a line. As she opened it to answer, a group of men emerged from the woods near town. Her father led, followed by two others. Lucy had never seen him with a gun before, and he held the barrel like it was hot to the touch.

The first man chatted with her father in an easy way. Tall and lanky, everything about him bespoke good nature and a respect for the firearm he carried. The second man frightened her more than the Indians ever could have. His heavy step, massive shoulders, and the way he dangled the gun from his hand made her want to crawl in the basket with Dodger and hide. When she thought of the rabbit, something poked at the back of her mind.

"Lucy!" Her father's voice cracked. He wanted to shake her, that was quite plain. Instead, he turned to the first man. "Sheriff," he said, "I'd like to introduce my wife." Her father turned a glare on Lucy that would have hushed an entire school. "And this is my daughter, Lucy."

"Pleased to meet you." Lucy dropped a curtsy.

"Give her a hiding, I would," said the other man.

Everyone stared at him. After a pause her father said, "And this is Mr. Altman."

Altman? Katherine's father? "Well, that explains a lot," Lucy said, not realizing she'd spoken aloud until she saw Altman's face.

"What did you say, girl?" he asked, stepping toward her.

Lucy clamped a hand over her mouth, horrified that she'd let her thoughts slip out. She didn't seem to have control over her eyes, either, as she couldn't help staring at Altman's teeth. From the looks of them, he shared his daughter's bad breath.

The sheriff leaned forward to ruffle Lucy's hair. "I know you've just stepped off the boat, but best not to wander about, young miss," he said. "There are wild things and rum runners all through these parts."

"I'm sorry, sir."

"I'd lock her up," said Altman, and spat for punctuation. "Teach 'er not to wander."

The sheriff gave Altman an odd look and invited Lucy to come down and play at his house one day with his four girls. *Highly unlikely*, Lucy thought, with the sheriff's daughter being Katherine's best friend—but she managed to keep that thought to herself.

"What was that man doing with you?" Lucy's mother asked, as they all watched Altman's back disappear into the forest.

"Best tracker in town," replied her father, setting the gun on the porch and pulling Lucy around to face him. The look in his eyes made her feel far worse than all her mother's scolding. She dropped her gaze and regarded the porch floor.

Then her mother reached to open the front door.

Lucy's insides swooned. She'd forgotten to put the lid back on the basket, and she'd left her bedroom door wide open. "Wait!" she yelled, as her mother reached for the doorknob.

CHAPTER 4

Going to Bed Hungry

"What in heaven's name?" Lucy's mother asked as she stepped into the kitchen and tried to find a safe place to put her feet. The coal scuttle had been kicked over and sooty tracks zigzagged across the long floorboards—just whitewashed yesterday. Black paw prints decorated dishcloths and napkins, and crocks of flour and oats had been knocked to the floor where they lay at crazy angles, cracked.

The footprints led to the oven, where her father found a quivering black ball with ears. Lucy scooped him out, getting soot all over herself in the process. Dodger was lucky the stove hadn't been lit, and Lucy was lucky her mother didn't put him in a pot and roast him for supper.

What was left of her Saturday was spent scrubbing footprints from the floors, washing aprons and cloths, and refilling the coal scuttle. When all her bones ached and she thought she would die from hunger, her father said, "Please tend to your friend, and take yourself off to bed."

Lucy hadn't eaten all day. Her mother would have relented by now, but her father's anger, though slower to ignite, burned fierce. He didn't offer to do their nightly reading in the parlor, or to come up and tell Lucy a story about teachers in faraway places. He didn't look at her at all.

After watching Dodger stuff himself with clover, she locked him in the chicken coop. Up in her room, she threw herself on her quilt—wishing she could eat the smell of biscuits and gravy drifting up the stairwell. After awhile, she rolled over and fell fast asleep with all her clothes on.

On Sunday, the Reverend Steele delivered a sermon dry as a ship's biscuit, but Lucy was grateful that a fine meal followed. At least there was no scrubbing. Her only problem with the Sabbath was that it was followed by Monday, and school.

Monday morning, Lucy woke early. She stuck out her jaw and reached for the only pair of stockings she had left—the fine ones. She wondered if the others were still tied to branches and twigs. She shivered. The dress she'd worn to the picnic was still moist from the boys splashing her on the way back. The other lay in her mother's mending basket, ripped and dirty after Lucy's frantic slide at the cliff. One work boot stood on the porch outside, caked in mud, and the other was at sea. She glared at the white ones, stained on top from Katherine's boot.

Nothing could have prepared her for the weather in Port Townsend, or those girls. Cliffs were cliffs, she didn't hold it against them. But girls could be nice, if they wanted to be. As she laced up the white boots, she dwelt again on the word *fun*.

Watching fireworks, spying on boys in the street, or simply sitting on the stoop with a friend back home—these things were fun. She decided to give Mr. Noah Webster's dictionary another chance.

fun: amusement or light-hearted pleasure
variation: funning
origin: late 1600s—a trick or a hoax, to make a fool of

Well, that much was true. Katherine was having fun making a fool of Lucy!

Lucy needed to talk things over with somebody. She found Dodger in a corner of the hutch, being pecked by sharp-clawed hens. She let herself in, and he didn't struggle when she picked him up. The thought crossed her mind that he was happy to be rescued. She set him on her knees and rubbed his velvety paws with her fingers.

She told him all about her first days, and how friendly the Indian girl had been. "You'd think, with all our differences, she would be the last one to help me." He hopped off to chew a clump of grass through the wire. "I wish there was a dictionary for people," she said. He turned one ear back, as though listening to her, but kept chewing. She laughed. He reminded her of her father when he was reading the paper but pretending to listen to her mother. "It would save so much time," she said. "You'd see if they were truly mean, and give up on ever being friends."

Their kitchen table had come with the house, a rough thing that snagged towels and fingers. The poor innocent who'd made it had also built the house for his fiancée. Lucy heard he'd gone all the way back to Scotland, only to find she'd gotten tired of waiting and married another, leaving him with an empty heart and home. Lucy wished her father had resisted the "romance of the place" and bought one closer to the center of town, like all the other families.

Breakfast started with a lecture and a scalded tongue from the lumpy porridge her father had made. Adding to her pain, she snagged her fingernail on the rough table and said a very unlady-like word.

"Lucy!" he said, "Watch your tongue, please, and listen to me for a moment. You may not go out anywhere alone," he said. "You will be accompanied to school. You will do your chores, and after school you will return to the house." Lucy looked up long enough to notice that he was wearing her mother's ruffled apron, and had to look down again to hide a smile.

"For how long?" she asked.

"Until your mother and I feel we can trust you again."

She felt the smile fade from her face. She'd been thinking a lot about the twins, hoping she might cross paths with them again. But she knew earning her freedom could take time. Her parents were more watchful and than they'd ever been in Boston. There, she was allowed to walk about freely with friends; sometimes even alone, if they knew where she was going.

After breakfast, she and her father went straight to the schoolhouse without any side trips for picking branches or feathers. They walked silently through the woods, and then the homes in the upper area of town. He offered no tales of heroic teachers, like her Auntie Alice who'd gone down the Welsh coal mines to save bright minds from the darkness.

The clapboard-sided school was perched at the edge of the bluff, near most of the students' houses and at the head of the stairs to the waterfront. When Lucy arrived, the whispers and laughter started with two girls outside and moved along with her into the one-room school. She knew she was once again overdressed, but why would that draw this much chatter?

Katherine sat at the back of the room, chewing on a tasty bit of news with the older girls. Lucy knew she was the object of Katherine's gossip and sat down in the first row, amazed at the fuss they were making. You'd think someone's barn had burned down, or a child had been dropped head-first down a well!

She looked around her. The school was tiny, compared to their old one in Boston, but she had to admit it wasn't terrible. She was surprised to find two large windows on each side, bathing the room with light. The floor was made up of solid boards (she'd been afraid it would be dirt) and the walls washed a clean white. A pot-bellied stove sat in one corner, unlit and looking cranky and ancient. The best part was the breeze flowing in through the open windows, carrying the taste of salty air, and so many sounds! Ships and bells and cargo, and the swish of waves rising up to them in their perch above the seaport.

She hoped to escape teasing when she went out for recess, but cries of "City Girl!" and "Got lost in your own back yard, eh?" greeted her.

"What?" Lucy asked, confused.

"Need a tracker to find the outhouse?" one of the boys asked, and then ran off making rude noises.

Lucy realized they must be talking about the sheriff having

to look for her. She busied herself weaving a crown of daisies for one of the kindergarteners. But though her fingers were busy, her ears couldn't stop listening. The girls stood in clusters, whispering and then bursting into peals of laughter. She heard her name, and *teacher's daughter*. Lucy found herself trembling with frustration, and went back inside. She picked up *Quotes of the Philosophers*, a huge book that was far too advanced for the likes of Katherine. She was tempted to "accidentally" drop it on Katherine's foot, but she was already in enough trouble with her father.

The only person in the school house was Matthias Bishop. Her father said Matthias got up at four to milk the cows. He studied furiously every minute he was at school, then left early when his father had finished his milk and cream deliveries. Lucy had noticed that all the girls sighed whenever Matthias walked by. At sixteen, he was just enough older than the rest of the boys to look like a man. In Lucy's short history of the place, Matthias hardly ever said a word and rarely looked up.

Today, he winked.

Lucy dropped the philosophers, and tried to look graceful as she picked them up again.

"Don't let them trouble you," he said.

"Who?" she asked.

He bent over his work again, and Lucy wondered if she'd imagined the wink. With his head down, she noticed how dark the skin was above his shirt collar. For some reason, she thought of the Indian boy in the meadow.

Matthias caught her looking at him. Mesmerized by the brown flecks in his sea green eyes, Lucy felt a blush kindle at the back of her neck and spread until her ears were aflame.

"They're just idle and bored," he said, looking amused. "They don't mean any real harm." Then he smiled. "My!" was all she could think. His teeth gleamed white in his sandy-brown face and he wore an expression of general good humor. His sleeves were rolled up and the muscles stood out on his forearms.

Lucy found herself smiling back at him. She was trying to think of something to say when the children tumbled back through the door, dropping hisses and taunts in Lucy's ear as they passed. This time, she didn't pay them any attention.

After school, her father pulled her aside. "Sweetheart, I have to finish some work here. I've asked some of the girls to take you down to town with them."

"Father," she hissed, watching Katherine stomp and fidget outside the door. "Please! I'll read in the corner, I'll scrub the floor... anything!"

"Go," he said. "For heaven's sake, Lucy, get some fresh air. It's lovely outside."

I'd rather be pickled in lemon juice and shoved in a jar, she wanted to say, but he'd already bent over his papers and wasn't responding to her eyes scorching the top of his head. She had no choice but to go.

Katherine struck out in the lead of the group of girls, and Lucy dragged along at the tail— trying to stay as far away from her as possible. Lucy suddenly remembered that her friend Emily had wanted, "details please, as soon as you arrive." What could she write? Katherine wasn't nice in any language, and the rest of the girls weren't much better. Matthias had smiled at her, but one smile wasn't enough to write home about. She'd begged Emily to visit, and didn't want to discourage her. Lucy decided she'd sketch a picture of town instead. Emily had always loved Lucy's drawings.

Most of the group had clattered half-way down the stairs already. Lucy paused by the railing at the top and considered. The biggest feature of the town had to be the bluff. It loomed above the waterfront, and the edge was so steep that anything with wheels had to drive all the way down to the end, past the Indian village, and then back along the road below. The settlers had built a long set of wooden stairs to connect "uptown" with the harbor below.

She looked down them. Most of the boys from school were milling around at the bottom.

A young lady shouldn't be seen clattering downstairs in her good dress, especially when boys were watching. Everyone knew that. But since few qualified for the word "civilized" here, Lucy supposed regular manners didn't apply. She picked up her skirts and ran down the steps, hurrying after the others.

At the bottom, the boys peeled off toward the docks. Lucy could bet they picked up bad words there, or pestered the sailors for stories about faraway places. If they asked, which they wouldn't because they'd never listen to a person in a dress, she'd tell them a sea voyage consisted of rats, mold, and heaving stomachs. And that most of your things got broken in high seas or destroyed by the damp. None too dreamy.

The girls didn't look back once to see if Lucy was still with them. She kicked a rock along the gutter. She hadn't played kick-the-can since she was small, but she was getting great satisfaction out of pretending it was Katherine's head. Bits of conversation drifted back to her from the two girls closest to her.

"Hey! Do you remember, about the scalp?"

Lucy looked up to see who'd spoken.

"Oh yes!" said a girl named Ruby who had pale skin, brick-red hair, and an imagination as wild as the horses on Zeus' chariot.

"The poor Colonel..." Ruby said.

Katherine was far ahead, but somehow she'd heard Ruby. She turned and drew her finger across her throat, lolling her tongue out the side of her mouth.

Lucy pulled Ruby aside. "What are you talking about?"

Ruby's eyes widened. "Didn't you know?" She twisted the hem of her dress between her fingers. "Well, Colonel Isaac Ebey... used to live over there at Ebey's Landing." She pointed to across the water to the island where they'd had their picnic. "It was the Indians."

The other girls nodded in agreement.

"That did what?" Lucy prompted.

"Why, took his scalp away!" said one of the girls, sending a tingling shiver cascading all down Lucy's back. So near?

"That is, after they chopped off his head," another said.

"But first they shot him, of course," yet another girl chimed in.

"All that?" Lucy asked. "Are you sure it wasn't several people combined into one story?"

They shook their heads, looking at her with big eyes. "Oh no!" said several at once. "This is certain-sure. It's been in the papers and all."

"Which Indians killed him?" asked Lucy. Her father had told her the Clallams were mostly peace-loving; but that disagreements or even battles sometimes happened between the tribes that lived in the territory.

The first girl shrugged. "I don't know. Do you?" She turned to Ruby.

"You know, Indians!" Ruby answered, as though that ended the matter.

"My dad says a raiding party—all the way down from the Queen Charlotte Islands," said Katherine from up in front, "and he should know!" Lucy shivered again, but this time at the thought of Katherine's father.

"Anyhow," said a girl, "they shot the Colonel over some grudge or another."

"*Before* they scalped him, of course," said Ruby. Under her breath, she added, "Thank goodness he wasn't still alive."

Lucy's stomach lurched. "That was a long time ago, right?"

"Oh, no," they said, shaking their heads. "A year or so."

"Five years."

"Two. I'm sure of it." The girls started squabbling over the details.

Katherine's voice rang out above the others. "It's six. Know how they found him?"

The others remained mute. Lucy couldn't help shaking her head no.

"Tripped over his headless body!" Katherine said, and stared right into Lucy's eyes, daring her to act squeamish.

"But the scalp... " said Ruby.

"Never got it!" said Katherine. "They sent a deputy to barter for it. I expect it'll be arriving any day now." She pulled a dust-covered piece of old jerky from her pocket and started chewing on it. "Dad gets all that stuff directly from the Sheriff."

In a daze, Lucy tried to match this story with the nice girl she'd seen in the meadow, and her twin brother—who'd seemed much like any other boy that came for lessons with her father. She wondered if there was a difference between the Indians who lived here and the ones who'd killed Ebey, or if there had been a particular reason for the attack. Deep in thought, she didn't notice that trouble was brewing up ahead.

"Look out for fleas, ladies!" Katherine bellowed. "Hey, teacher's daughter. Come here!"

CHAPTER 5

Saying the Wrong Thing

Lucy halted in the middle of the street. She'd lost her kicking rock, and her white boots squelched as she pulled them out of the muck. She trudged toward Katherine and the other girls, who stood outside one of the most important buildings in the settlement.

The trading post squatted on a pier over the water and was built of weathered boards. Fur pelts hung from hooks around the door, which was crowned with a large set of antlers. There were barrels of goods stacked along the side walls, right up to the low roof. The Indian girl who'd helped Lucy catch Dodger stood next to the door. She'd fixed her gaze down in the dirt.

"Can't even talk, I bet," sneered Katherine. "Can you talk English?" She yelled in the ear of the girl, who stood as tall as Katherine but had shrunk in on herself. So small that Lucy might not have recognized her. Lucy froze at the back of the group, feeling sick at the way Katherine was treating the girl.

Everyone else managed to laugh at Katherine's comments, even if their voices sounded hollow, but Lucy couldn't laugh at the only girl who'd been nice to her. Katherine stood with her hands on her hips, staring at Lucy, then the girl. "You kind of remind me of each other—neither of you can speak up." A few snickers escaped from the other girls.

Lucy knew she was expected to join in. Agreement was needed to stay out of trouble.

"Bet she has bad breath!" Katherine taunted, which made Lucy snort, considering the mouth that formed the words. Too late, Lucy realized that her laugh might sound like she agreed with Katherine. The Indian girl's head came up. A frown creased her forehead and her eyes searched Lucy's, while the others pressed in on them like a tightening noose.

"Well, what do you have to say?" Katherine demanded, poking Lucy hard.

"Me?" Lucy felt the noose draw in as she searched for a way to sidestep Katherine's challenge under the steady gaze of the Indian girl.

"Yes, you!" Katherine said. "You an Indian lover, like that Judge Swan?"

Lucy shrank back, her shoulder aching where Katherine had jabbed her. The taunts and whispers and pokes of the past days piled up inside. She wanted to lash out at someone, to break the hold of all those pairs of eyes. The words rushed out of her in a scornful tone, "Me, an Indian lover? Why ever would you think something stupid like that?"

She'd meant to counter Katherine, to take the opposite view, but the instant the words left her lips she knew they were horribly wrong.

"Well, well," said Katherine, nodding her approval. "Little Book Girl can talk after all." She went into the store, pulling girls after her like a peacock trailing tail feathers.

Just like that, the tension slackened. Lucy could feel it in the little laughs and explosive breaths that escaped from the others' mouths, all but the silent girl by the door. Lucy avoided looking her way as she pushed into the store behind the rest, but she could feel the Indian girl's eyes on her as she let the screen door fall closed.

Inside, light fell through a row of rough windows along one side of the narrow store and lit up sacks of flour and piles of striped wool blankets. Reflections from the waves outside rippled on the ceiling. A counter along the other side was covered in glass jars full of tobacco plugs, tallow candles, jerked meat, and even hair ribbons and hard candies. One girl took Lucy's arm and asked her what kind of candy she liked best, but Lucy's mind wasn't on candy. Maybe the girl outside hadn't really understood what Lucy was talking about, she told herself. Maybe her English wasn't that good.

Katherine glared at the girl with Lucy, and she dropped Lucy's arm and went back over to the other side of the store. They reminded Lucy of a flock of chickens: peck, peck, peck... run, run, run! Chickens, she reminded herself, were not very bright. She stood alone, fidgeting with a saddle buckle.

Mr. Cady, the owner of the trading post, was arguing with a tall Indian.

"Prince George, you must pay for your goods!" he sputtered, and pounded his silver cash register. The bell pinged and the drawer popped open.

The Indian gathered up a pile of goods, including a fistful of tobacco twists and some canned pork, a blanket and some socks. He made his way through the girls, and they scattered as he tossed a parting comment over his shoulder at the owner.

"I'll pay you for this when you pay me for my land!" the Indian said. "Right here, about where your store sits." He pointed at the floor. "Pay me for that."

"We've been through all that!" The owner was turning red. "Be reasonable!" He let out a huge sigh as the Indian shrugged and left, letting the screen slam shut behind him.

Lucy fought her way to the counter. "Who was that?"

"That was Prince George, brother to the Chief Clallam," said Mr. Cady, "and you'd best stay out of his way."

Lucy watched through the screen as the girl got into a canoe with the man. Prince? Was the girl a princess then? She wasn't like any of the ones Lucy had read about... plain clothes and no shoes. But there was something—a way about her—especially when she'd given Lucy the basket.

For good or ill, the pattern was set. Every day after school, the girls left together—with Katherine at their lead and Lucy having no choice but to follow. It wasn't so bad if she stayed in the back.

They meandered around town, buying candy here or a spool of thread there, while Lucy was filled in on what to avoid. She was told to stay out of the way of: drunken sailors, drunken loggers down from the hills, and drunken prospectors gathering up supplies for the Alaska gold rush. But most of all avoid Tate Altman, they said, when Katherine was out of earshot. He hated children, and the bruises on Katherine's arms served as quiet witnesses.

Lucy didn't see the Indian girl again. She often wondered about her, but she was glad to avoid another scene. She hoped she'd have the courage to stick up for the girl with Katherine if the same thing happened again, but who knew what would come out of her mouth?

Her father had still not loosened his restrictions, though Lucy asked him every day. She was thoroughly sick of being marched through uptown like a prisoner on parade, then through the woods to her front porch and her mother. It was humiliating!

One day, Katherine stopped at the beginning of the path that threaded the trees to Lucy's house. She dared Lucy to walk through alone. "If you're not chicken!" Katherine said, standing so close that Lucy could smell her breath—something like tinned sardines mixed with sauerkraut. At this point, nothing could be worse than Katherine.

"I'm not afraid," said Lucy, meeting the girl's stare.

"Sure the cougars won't get you?" Katherine taunted.

Lucy laughed. She'd seen no bears or giant white-headed birds. She shrugged in a devil-may-care way, and turned to the woods. But Ruby dropped a very different worry into her mind. "Wait!" she said, looking alarmed. She laid a hand on Lucy's arm, restraining her. "Best watch out for that Injun they chased out of the pharmacy the other day!"

"What?" asked Katherine, miffed at being late with any news.

Ruby's eyes glinted with satisfaction. "My father saw him come tearing out the back of the pharmacy with a knife in his hand."

"Yeah?" breathed one of the girls.

"Yeah!" said Ruby, breathing on her nails and then polishing them on her dress. "Of course I know these things, my father being the sheriff."

"Spit it out, already!" said Katherine. Lucy could see that Ruby was enjoying herself.

"Well…that thief was going through the store room right next to the pharmacist's bedroom. Would have took everything if the pharmacist hadn't woke up. Would have done more, if he hadn't yelled his head off." She drew a finger across her throat.

For such a mild girl, she sure likes gore, thought Lucy, staring at Ruby.

She wanted to think that Ruby's imagination had run away with her again, but something crawled up her spine: a sense that this might be the truth. After all, Ruby's father was the sheriff. But Katherine's twisted smile clearly said that Lucy was a chicken. She couldn't back down now.

"I'm sure he's long gone," Lucy said, trying to keep her voice confident.

"Who knows?" said Katherine, with a shrug, and left. Ruby followed, glancing back at Lucy with a mix of curiosity and guilt on her face.

Lucy hadn't gone far when she heard someone approaching. She jumped off the path, behind a cedar tree big enough for ten children to link their arms around. From both sides of her, footsteps drew near. An argument started, and Lucy couldn't resist peeking out. She spied Prince George from the trading post, the Indian girl's brother, and a man with a jagged scar down one arm—mostly likely the one from the pharmacy incident.

Lucy held her breath, and tried to hear through the pulse pounding in her ears.

The Prince held out a sack that made a clinking sound. The boy shook his head and they argued more. Prince George handed the sack to the mean-looking Indian and turned to go. As he was leaving, Prince George stared straight at Lucy and gave her a slow wink.

She pulled back behind the tree, pressed her face into the rough bark, and waited.

Nothing. Not even any talking.

She needed to see, under the cover of a branch...

The scarred Indian stood close to the boy, inches from his face, and his expression made Lucy shrink back against the tree and stay there. After a long moment, some twigs snapped and the clinking sound moved off deeper into the woods.

The boy let out his breath in a deep sigh. Lucy waited, listening to all the small sounds of the forest. It was so still, and not a breath of wind. As her heart quieted, she worried about another problem, which was the result of not wanting to use the stinky outhouse at school.

Something stabbed her sharply in the ribs. Lucy let out a yelp, and crossed her legs so she wouldn't have an accident. The Indian boy dangled a stick from his hand. A fringe of dark hair fell across his forehead, partially hiding his eyes. A dimple, like a dot at the end of a sentence, creased one side of his face. Later, Lucy would think that the boy could be read two different ways, depending on which side of his face you saw—the dimpled or the flat.

"Uncle saw you," he said slowly.

"What are you doing here?" Lucy demanded, climbing out and examining the bow, arrows, and a dead rabbit on the path. She bent over to study the animal, glad it wasn't Dodger.

His eyes asked the same question of her, making her realize that she'd been caught spying, and alone. She wondered if Indian girls always had to be escorted everywhere like settler girls, or at least like settler Lucy.

The boy raised an eyebrow. After gathering up his things, he motioned for her to go first, which was the last thing Lucy wanted. But what else could she do? She stepped ahead, toward her house, her mind rapidly turning over what she'd just seen. Was he dangerous? Prince George didn't look dangerous, especially after the wink. But the third man was a mean piece of work, certain sure.

Within sight of her house, she stopped and turned. "Goodbye, and, uh... thank you," she said and smiled, then frowned. *Why am I thanking him for scaring me silly?*

The boy shrugged. As she turned to go, Lucy thought she caught the flicker of a smile on his face. She ran across the clearing and then forced herself to take the steps slowly, feeling his eyes on her. When she glanced back, he was still there under the trees. But when she came in and peered through the window curtains, he was gone.

That night, Lucy dreamed of shadowy figures in the woods, scars, scalps, and war canoes. A large dictionary snapped shut every time she tried to read it, and a giant finger kept jabbing her. The face of the rabbit girl kept drifting through—with her eyes turned down somewhere below her. Each time she passed, Lucy was left with a sense of lingering sorrow.

CHAPTER 6

Trying to Make Amends

Lucy woke with a headache and the inklings of an idea, grateful that it was Saturday. At breakfast, she went to work on her mother. "What if a girl gave me something and I forgot to say thank you? What if I borrowed something and never returned it?"

"You know as well as I how to treat a friend, Lucy," said her mother. "You'd say a late thank you and attach a gift." She worked at her bread dough. "There are some nice families here. I hope you're making friends?" She smiled, but her skin had that chalky look Lucy'd been noticing lately. The last thing her mother needed to hear was that Lucy had managed to be only a barnacle on the surface of Katherine's group (which included every girl within a twenty-mile radius). They were like clams at low tide—closed up tight.

"Well, sort of," she said.

"You could invite them here," her mother said. "We could make jam tarts!"

Lucy tried to imagine Katherine in their kitchen. *No thank you!* And there was no way to ask anyone else without Katherine inviting herself along. Lucy thought of cooking-baking parties back home, with the girls' hair frizzled by the heat and their fingers sticky with jam. They rolled and cut, and chattered like magpies. Afterwards, they sold the cookies to neighbor ladies for a penny a dozen and stuffed themselves with the leftovers.

She asked if they could leave out the rest of the town, and her mother gave in. But with only the two of them, and no one nearby to exclaim over the perfect hearts Lucy cut in the middle, or the bright red jam peeking through, it didn't feel the same. She mostly made them because her mother was trying so hard to be cheerful. Still, they might be useful.

Soon after the cookies were done, Lucy's mother wilted, and Lucy had to do all the washing up alone. She felt incomplete. If you didn't have anyone to eat the cookies with, what was the point of making them? She visited the chickens and tried to cradle one on her lap, but they didn't like being held. Not yet. She'd tamed all manner of wild things, but these western animals seemed particularly hard to befriend. She rubbed her hand where one had pecked her.

Hearing a noise, Lucy spied the Indian boy at the edge of the clearing. She came out of the chicken coop, straightened her dress and smoothed her hair. He stood so still, she wondered if she'd conjured him from her worrying dreams. Then he turned to leave.

"Wait!" she said, glad she'd started on her plan already.

He hesitated.

"Where's your sister?"

"Why?" he asked, crossing his arms and glaring at her. She noticed that he was wearing the same clothes as the day they'd first met, including the lack of shirt.

Lucy thought quickly. This might be Providence wrapped up in a shirtless boy. "I wanted to say thank you, to give her something." The boy stopped to consider, and a breath of hope stirred in her that her luck might at last be changing.

He put his fingers in his mouth and whistled. From up the path, the girl peeked out. Lucy could find no hint of welcome in her face. She knew she deserved a cold greeting, or none at all.

"Please," said Lucy, beckoning them closer. The girl swayed as though about to respond, but stayed where she was. "Wait here!" Lucy said, and ran up the stairs for some cookies. When she came back, the girl had drawn a little nearer. Her twin hovered near his sister, with his hand resting on the bow slung over his shoulder.

Lucy offered the plate of cookies. They both took one, but they seemed unsure. "Eat! They're good!" Lucy urged. This definitely did not match the scene she'd imagined, with them all sitting down together on the front step.

"Lucy, what are you doing?" called her mother, halting on her way past the door.

"Mother, this is the girl I was telling you about."

Her mother, who'd just woken from a nap, stared at the shirt-less boy.

"You know, the one I owed a favor to?" Lucy prompted. "I was going to take her some cookies, but look, they've come. Isn't that lucky?"

"Oh! Well, yes!" Her mother's gaze rested on the girl as she came down the steps. She offered her hand. "I'm Lucy's mother."

The girl did not take her hand, but after a minute she spoke. "I'm Kwilcid."

"Pleased to meet you..." her mother said, clearly not sure how to cope with the Indian name. "Say it again for me?"

"If it's easier for you, you can call me Quill—like a pen." The brother did not offer his name or his hand.

"Pleased to meet you, Quill," Lucy's mother said, letting her hand fall to her side.

Lucy could feel herself beginning to sweat under her dress. *This is going about as smoothly as a cart with square wheels.*

Her mother said, "Lucy!" and Quill laughed.

"Did I say that out loud?" she asked, and groaned. Things escaped from her thoughts and out her mouth at the worst times. "I'm Lucy," she said. Quill smiled, then nibbled a bite of the cookie. Lucy couldn't tell from the girl's expression if she liked it, or was simply being polite.

The twins didn't leave but they wouldn't sit, and Lucy's mother was beginning to look pale again. Lucy brought out her last two items. She gave Dodger to Quill to hold, and felt the mood warm between them. Then Lucy made the mistake of trying to return the basket.

Quill pushed it away. "I would not take back a gift!"

"But it's yours!" Lucy started to sweat again. The boy had moved toward the forest.

"Here, please," Lucy offered a jar of ruby-red crabapple jelly. Most of the jars had broken on the ship, and her mother looked startled when she saw one of their last ones leaving. But she didn't say anything.

Quill held the jelly up to the light, and it glowed ruby red. "Thank you," she said, dipping her head ever so slightly.

Princess, Lucy thought, and let out her breath.

A few days later, she was gathering eggs and whispering to Dodger, who sat under the edge of her skirt, hiding from the chickens. She heard a soft whistle nearby. Quill hovered at the edge of the woods, half in and half out of the shade. Her face was dappled with leaf shadows.

"Hello, Quill," Lucy said quietly, afraid she'd disappear.

"Hello, Lucy!" Quill replied. She moved out of the shadows. "We go tomorrow, to the little island." She pointed back, toward the meadow beach. "Auntie says, 'Come gather with us.'"

Lucy stepped out of the coop, closing it carefully. "With you? Truly?" This was Lucy's first real invitation. Katherine now ditched her at the top of the stairs each day with the order, "Don't follow us." None of the others seemed ready to risk Katherine's anger by joining Lucy. So, she wandered uptown alone until enough time had passed to go home. Every day, she suffered the same humiliation.

She yearned to accept Quill's invitation, but she was sure her mother would say no. How could she explain without hurting Quill's feelings?

Quill waited patiently. "We go to gather," she searched for the word, "straw-berries."

"Berries?" Lucy's mouth watered. "I don't know if I can," she said, "but I'll definitely try!"

Quill nodded again, smiling broadly enough that her dimple appeared. Lucy watched her disappear into the trees, and called out a belated, "Thank you!" But got no reply.

Berries! She'd seen the cedar plank houses at the far end of the beach downtown, with smoke curling out of their roofs. Now it occurred to her that she had no idea what went on inside those homes—how the Indians cooked or what they ate, other than the silver-sided salmon that ran so plentifully in northwest waters. The salmon was all right, but strawberries!

At dinner, Lucy tried to sound casual. "Quill wants me to go pick wild strawberries tomorrow." The look on her mother's face prompted Lucy to add, "You could use some fresh fruit, for canning!"

"It's one thing to have the child visit here," her mother began. "She seems perfectly… nice. But we don't know her family. And I suppose this would be in a canoe?" Canoes were the main way people got around, with thick forests and few roads, but her mother didn't trust them. Deep inside, Lucy knew her mother's worries were reasonable, but out loud she said, "The other girls go all over the place alone, or in canoes—like Katherine Altman."

"Really, Lucy! Do you see them going anywhere with children from the tribe?"

She had to admit she hadn't.

"And Katherine Altman is no role model, her being without a mother and all."

"I'll go with her," said her father, stepping in. "I'll do some collecting for the Judge."

Her mother's face went sour. She didn't like Judge Swan for some reason. Lucy excused herself and started up the stairs. Time to let her father work his magic on her mother.

"You could use the quiet. You need to rest," Lucy heard her father say in a tense voice, and she paused midway up the steps.

"Shhh. James. She'll hear you! Lucy's not stupid."

Lucy tiptoed back down a few steps.

There were murmurs. "But when?" His voice rose. "I think she should know."

"I'll tell her," said her mother. "I will tell her...later."

"Later...something goes wrong, what then?"

Her mother's voice, "... things so difficult at school... not bringing any girls home to visit. She has no one to talk to. Let's wait a bit."

Lucy sat down in the stairwell.

So, her mother knew perfectly well that she was struggling. But why did she need rest? Lucy hadn't heard her coughing, or seen her spitting blood. People with consumption usually wasted away, like the girl in Boston who'd died; but her mother hadn't gotten skinny, though pale as flour paste. Back home, some of the ladies took Carter's Little Liver Pills for their constitutions, but her mother had never used them. A shadow passed across her mood. Lucy had thought the chalky look was from the lack of light in this cloudy town, or working hard to make their new house comfortable. She wanted to know, but didn't dare ask: What ailed her mother?

On their way to the island, Lucy was very aware of the young man at the back of the boat. She tried to school her expression into one of serious thought, as she feared acting too excited would make her look like a small child. But she soon lost the battle. She felt her face relax into a wide smile in response to everything around her.

She savored every detail of her first canoe ride: the morning sun pooled like oil on the smooth cradles of water, the paddle slicing through swells that gently lifted and then dropped the boat. She loved how the seals streaked along, keeping time with them, their silvery bodies gliding, then disappearing, to pop up a little farther away.

One seal pup came up right next to Quill's brother. It had watery eyes and quivering whiskers. He flicked it away with his paddle, but it popped up again beyond the boy's reach. They played the game over and over again, bringing the first laugh Lucy had heard from him. The seal's silver fur, the water's shivering surface...everything seemed to reflect light into Quill's brother, bringing him to life.

That morning, they had met on the beach by the meadow. Her father had asked Quill's brother his name, which brought the short reply, "Henry." Her father asked if Henry also had a native name. "Quill tells me her English name is Ann," he said.

"Just Henry," the boy replied, clearly unwilling to say his other name. His voice had cracked on the second syllable. Lucy had been puzzling over the twins' age. She'd thought they were older, but most of the boys in Boston with the voice-cracking problem were about her own age—fifteen at the most.

She looked up to see the object of her thoughts staring at her, and looked down again.

Their canoe carried Henry in the back, the two girls in the middle, and Lucy's father in the front, facing the back of the boat. He turned his attention to Quill. "Where did you learn your English?" he asked, leaning forward. *Poor Quill!* Lucy knew what it was like to suffer her father's curiosity, and felt a little worried about how her new friend would respond.

Quill leaned away. "From my Auntie's man," she said. "He is a trapper."

"Is it that auntie?" Her father nodded toward a very old woman in the next canoe.

Quill laughed. "Not *that* auntie!"

"But her man taught you English?"

"A little," Quill said, frowning, "but not good."

"It sounds very good to me," he said, and smiled.

Quill shifted in her seat. She said something so softly, Lucy could hardly hear her. Then she turned away, trailing her hand through the smooth water. The drops that fell from her fingers looked like crystals on a chandelier, shimmering in the morning air.

"What do you wish?" Lucy whispered, as she watched the drops fall, one by one, from Quill's fingertips.

Quill tucked her hand under the blanket. "I wish to go to school."

School? If you asked most girls, they'd say, "I wish for dozens of dresses," or, "I wish for a handsome beau." No one Lucy knew would say *school*. Well, except Lucy herself, and maybe Matthias.

She waited for her father to ask Quill to join them in the schoolhouse, as he did with every other youngster in town. If they didn't come to school, he searched them out in their parents' fields or down in the holds of ships. He must have heard Quill's wish, with his ears trained to catch whispers from the back of the classroom.

But he said nothing. Lucy sat back, puzzled. Surely Quill qualified as one of those children "growing wild with the sailors and miners," they'd come all this way to educate? Wasn't that why he'd given up his post at a famous school and taken ship alone, hoping his family could join him later? Why she and her mother had braved moldy bread, Cape Horn, storms that broke most of her mother's china, and even a sailor fight that ended in a man drowned? Why she'd left her cat behind, and all the wild animals she'd nursed back to health?

She decided to give him a little help. "She could come to school!" she said.

As Quill watched Lucy's father, the dreamy look faded from her face.

He stared back toward Port Townsend and sighed. Finally, he said, "Couldn't your uncle the trapper teach you?"

Lucy noticed Henry's hands then. His grip on the paddle was white-knuckled, and the dimple in his cheek had flattened out.

"Auntie's man does not read English," said Quill, after a long pause. "No one in our house reads."

Her father's silence clamped a lid on Lucy's hope for company in the schoolhouse, and he did not ask her any more questions. The seal popped up again, but Henry ignored it.

CHAPTER 7

A Day Away, Together

When they landed, the men pulled spears with sharp-looking points from their canoes. Lucy thought of poor Mr. Ebey and shivered.

"For fish!" Quill said, following her gaze. Then she raised her voice, "But Henry won't get any." Her brother made a face at his sister, then flashed a smile at Lucy that startled a flush into her cheeks. He turned his back on them, slipped the suspenders from his shoulders and pulled his shirt off, tossing it on the sand. Lucy watched the muscles ripple under the skin on his back as he hefted the spear.

"Berries!" said Quill, poking Lucy in the ribs.

Lucy felt glad her father had followed Quill's uncle. He would not approve of her gawping at a half-naked boy. Quill called for Lucy to follow, and she did. But somehow her head seemed to crane over her shoulder while her body went forward.

The small island resembled a child with wild hair—flat-topped, with sandy slopes around the sides and grass sticking out on top. Lucy climbed up behind Quill and found a gentle meadow spread in front of her, a bowl filled with grasses and low plants. Children dotted the field like puffs of cotton in their dresses, stuffing their plump cheeks with fruit. One little girl stared at Lucy with huge eyes. Quill whispered to her, and the girl went back to plucking berries.

The berries Lucy knew were pampered and watered and then brought to the market, or sold by the Berry Lady—with her red dress and her call of, "Strawberries, Strawberries, fat and fine! For the best, come try mine!" Lucy had to bend close to find these small wild ones. She plucked one, and the flavor exploded inside her mouth. It was the first fresh fruit she'd had in months. "Oh yum," she murmured happily, closing her eyes and tilting her face to the sun. She listened to the bees buzzing, and the knot that had coiled tight in her middle began to fade. When she opened her eyes, Quill's basket was half full. "How did you do that so quickly? And what will you do with them?" Lucy asked, putting a few into her own.

"Eat them. What do *you* do with food?"

"I meant... "

"We dry them," said Quill, sitting back and popping a hand-ful of berries into her mouth.

"We will make jelly!" said Lucy, "and jelly, and jelly!" She felt hot just thinking about all the boiling and steaming that went into putting up fruit.

"Like the jelly you gave me?" asked Quill. "Auntie liked the col-or. She put it on a shelf to remember your kindness." Quill beamed at Lucy, then returned to poking among the plants.

What would you give someone, if you owed them? Lucy knew she wouldn't have given Quill anything if she hadn't felt so ashamed of what happened with Katherine. An apology needed to leave her mouth, but she couldn't find the words, and she didn't want to in-terrupt the contentment of the day.

When they returned to the beach, the men were standing next to piles of shimmering silver fish. Her father struggled to hoist a line of them longer than he was tall. "Look at this!" he said.

"Did you catch them?" Lucy asked. Several of the men covered their mouths and coughed. Her father shook his head and laid the fish down, pointing at Prince George.

"Take some," said the Prince, gesturing toward the overflow-ing pile.

"Why, thank you!" her father said, then started to say some-thing else; but the man had turned his back. Today, the Prince didn't wink, and he didn't seem very talkative.

"Why doesn't he like us?" Lucy whispered to Quill.

Quill shrugged her shoulders, but she looked uncomfortable.

Her father had left his sketch book open on the sand. Lucy looked more closely. Two different hands had been at work on the pages. She recognized her father's style in the drawing of Henry with a spear in his hand, aiming. In another of his sketches, a great blue heron stared into the water at a fish. There was something similar in the fierce attention of boy and bird, and she could see why he'd placed them side by side. Her father's sketches were detailed and straight.

On the opposite page, a fish thrashed—as if ready to jump off the page. The pencil strokes were bold, wild and rounded. "Who did these?" Lucy wondered aloud. Quill pointed at Henry.

"He's really good!" Lucy said. She felt Quill's eyes on her. Blushing, she bent her head to study the canoes, men with spears, and the whiskered face of a seal. In all of them, Henry had captured the same sense of life as with the salmon. "Amazing!" said Lucy.

"Maybe Henry should sketch you?" Quill asked, her dimples flashing.

Lucy felt her face burn. "Shouldn't we be helping with…something?" she asked.

Only later did she realize that her father had finally persuaded Henry to speak with him, but through sketches instead of words. She'd never thought much about her father's talent: his ability to get almost any student to work with him. He and Henry had been talking about fishing and the sea with their pencils. Given time, she knew he'd get Henry to talk with him as well. But why hadn't he invited him to school?

At the end of the beach, women pried shellfish off rocks in the water. Several wore clips in their hair—made of inky black stone inlaid with silver and blue shell. Ribbons of seaweed danced around their ankles. The boys at school had warned Lucy of vicious sharks in the shallows. She looked around her at the faces of the women—some looking down on their work, some laughing and talking, the younger ones splashing each other—and figured she could chalk that up to another tall tale.

An old woman wore a tunic of rough material and a cone-shaped hat that looked like tree bark, which shaded her face. Lucy noticed her round back and the sureness with which she pried and moved along the rocks, flipping the little shells into a big basket. Her work went quickly, but there was no sense of rush about her—rather something timeless. The sun had moved higher in the sky and the island didn't offer even a shrub for shade. Lucy grew hot and envied the woman's bare feet in the tide pool. She wished her mother's last sentence hadn't been: "Stay out of the water!"

The woman pointed toward the cliff at the top of the island and handed Quill a basket. She bowed, took the basket from the woman with both hands and led Lucy toward the cliff. Lucy groaned, but followed. She'd make very sure she didn't get near the edge of this one.

Halfway up, Lucy stopped to dump sand out of her boots and shucked off her stockings as well. She wiggled her toes in the sand, and decided to leave them that way. She couldn't bear to force them back into the hot boots.

"Hold my feet," said Quill as soon as Lucy reached the top. Taking her ankles, Lucy leaned back hard while the girl eased herself down to dangle over the cliff's face. Remembering the feeling of a cliff crumbling under her feet, Lucy stayed away from the edge. "Ow!" said Quill, and Lucy realized her terror had transferred into her hands. She tried to ease her grip without letting go; but kept imagining her sweaty hands slipping and Quill plunging to the rocks below.

Small black birds dived at them as Quill gathered eggs, rolling them up over the lip of the cliff. "Lower!" she kept saying. Lucy peered over at the rocks and felt her breath stop. By the time Quill came back up with a little nest in her hands, Lucy's arms were quivering and she felt dizzy with fear. They sat down to rest, with

Quill kicking her legs over the side and Lucy cross-legged, planted on firm ground nearby.

Quill fished two strawberries out of her pocket and handed one to Lucy.

"How did you keep those from getting squished?" Lucy asked.

"Old S'Klallam trick!" Her dimples flashed and so did Lucy's suspicions that Quill was practicing on her, like the boys with their tales of giant birds. The breeze fanned Lucy's hot cheeks as the sun played across the water before them: ruffled, green, smooth, icy white. Quill had come up over the cliffside looking so happy, and Lucy thought she understood why. While she hated the edge, the wind and sky got into you up here. Quill turned to her with a grin, and Lucy decided to risk a few questions that had been rolling around in her mind.

CHAPTER 8

Boys and other Puzzles

"If Prince George is your uncle." Lucy asked, "Does that make you a princess?"

"I do not know about *princess*,'" Quill said in a matter-of-fact tone. "Prince George's brother—Chits-a-ma-hun (you call him Chetzmoka)—is our chief. He's also my other uncle. I sleep in his house."

"You live with him? Truly?"

Quill laughed. "Many people live with my uncle. We make room. Like when a cousin died—his Tsimshian wife and three children from her other husband came to live with us."

"That's a lot of people!" said Lucy.

"Our houses are large, especially our winter houses," said Quill. "You should come see mine!"

Lucy didn't know how to answer. Those who socialized too closely with the tribe (like Judge Swan) were not well thought-of by some in town; and the S'Klallam village in particular seemed to stir up ill feeling. Lucy's father was hired and paid by the town. She'd have to ask her mother's permission, and she was pretty sure what the answer would be.

"Are you unwell?" Quill asked.

Lucy realized she was about to miss a golden opportunity with Quill being so talkative. "No, I'm quite fine, thank you. But concerning your family—your *whole* family lives with your uncle?" she asked. Quill nodded and Lucy continued, "You and Henry and… your parents?"

Quill yanked a piece of oat grass from the turf and shredded it slowly with her fingers. Lucy watched her, mesmerized. "My mother was the chief's sister," Quill finally said, "but she is gone." Her voice held a tone like a door closing and Lucy knew better than to press. "Time to go down," Quill said, standing.

Lucy followed her, mulling over what she'd said. '*She is gone.*' Did that mean dead? And what about Quill's father?

Onboard the *Icarus* everything had been moist, and Lucy had started to feel moldy too. That feeling hadn't changed much during her first wet weeks in Port Townsend; not until today. As she slid down the back side of the cliff, she could feel the dry warmth of the sand pulsing up through her bare feet. She lifted her skirts and ran down the slope. Her feet were flying and her dress flapping around her legs. Suddenly, she was going too fast. Quill's back loomed in front of her, and she hardly had time to yell, "Look out!" before she crashed into her. Quill tripped and they tumbled in a tangle of arms and legs, rolling to a stop.

All activity on the beach stopped as the girls untangled themselves. Then Henry pointed and started laughing. Lucy looked down to find circles of egg-yolk blooming on her dress, and her embarrassment gave fire to her fingers. She found a whole egg and launched it at Henry, who was too surprised to move out of the way. The egg exploded all over his feet, and it was her turn to laugh at the expression on his face.

Quill hooted at her twin while Lucy went to the water's edge to wash, certain her mother would skin her alive if she arrived home with egg all over her clothes. Teachers, she'd been reminded many a time, are practically beggars, and clothes do not grow on trees. She imagined all the trees in Port Townsend sprouting aprons, overalls, mittens, and petticoats, and laughed.

After a moment, Henry joined her. They stood, side by side, watching the surf swoosh in and out around their feet, hers pink with cold; his yellow with egg. As he rinsed the yolk off, she wondered what to say. She hadn't been around boys much, other than tutoring the five-year-olds with their math facts.

Before she could think of anything to say, he left, muttering something. She thought he said, "Thanks a lot!" but it could also have been, "Nice shot!"

The aunties boiled the mussels, clams, and china hats they'd gathered for lunch. The limpets, as her father had called them, were sweet and chewy. His slurps told her he was enjoying more of the large oysters, eaten raw. They'd felt slimy to Lucy, and she thought hers might come back up. She did not like the sickly green color of their insides, either.

Henry appeared, pointed at the china hats, and said, "tunsu'etc."

"Tawn saw etch," repeated Lucy, trying to twist her tongue around the sounds.

"No, tunsu'etc," he said, his eyes on a level with hers as he crouched near her in the sand.

She tried a few times more. Finally, she said, "tun-su-etc," softly. He smiled his approval. Pointing at the eggs, he said, "You throw hard!" His head was tilted, as if asking a question.

"Crows," she said.

"Crows?"

"They ate some baby squirrels, in my yard," said Lucy.

"Of course," said Henry, in a matter-of-fact voice.

"It was awful!" Lucy recalled the pitiful sound the tiny squirrels made when their mother was killed by a cat, then the way the sound changed as crows grabbed a baby from the nest and pulled it apart. Her father wouldn't let her interfere. "Lucy, you'd kill yourself trying to get up that tree!"

Lucy had developed a strong throwing arm during the bad times in their house. Each time they lost a tiny soul, her father would walk with Lucy until her mother mended. They'd wind their way through the streets and always end by skipping rocks at the sea wall. He never spoke about her mother's health, or the little ones who'd left her body too soon, but the rock-throwing seemed to help them both.

She realized Henry was waiting for her to speak. "I threw

rocks at the crows to keep them from eating the babies," she said. "It worked, but I couldn't reach them after. The babies starved."

"Crows need to eat too," Henry said, "...and starving is a worse death."

Lucy felt sure he spoke of more than squirrels. They both fell silent and she watched him walk back to stand by his uncle. He was slighter of build than Prince George, but had a lean power. Lucy wondered what these men who caught their food with spears, bows and guns thought of her father. All the other fathers in town hunted elk and deer, bringing back antlers. Almost every barn had a rack of them over the door. Lucy thought they should hang a book outside her own house.

Near the canoes, Quill drilled holes through the china hat shells with a nail. She asked Lucy to string them on a piece of twine. Her fingers knew this: like braiding silk threads or hair for wearing a cameo. All around them, women packed berries and layered fish in beds of seaweed. They used large baskets, flat baskets, open baskets, covered baskets—even water-tight baskets for boiling their eggs.

Lucy watched the procession of baskets down to the canoes.

"We are always weaving!" said Quill wryly, but then her voice took on a different tone. "I am..." She started, but then stopped.

"You are what?" Lucy asked.

"I was going to say I am a good weaver, but that would be wrong," Quill said.

"Why?" Lucy asked. "If you've worked hard to learn something?"

Quill shook her head. "Everyone works; I should not speak only of myself." She dropped a loop of shells over Lucy's head. Lucy did the same for Quill, feeling they'd made a pact of sorts, like when the boys spit on their hands and shook.

They joined Lucy's father, who waited by the water with his shoes tied around a very sun-burned neck. Lucy settled herself into the gently bobbing canoe. Henry was about to push off when she remembered. "My shoes!"

Lucy stood, making the boat rock crazily, and tried to step out.

"I have to get them!" she said, as panic spread through her at the thought of facing her mother without them. Henry shook his head no, and Quill pulled her back down to sit.

"You don't understand," Lucy said, feeling the tears fill her eyes. "I have no shoes now."

The twins exchanged a look, and Lucy thought they were thinking how bird-brained she was until Henry reached into the front of the canoe, pulled out her sandy boots and dropped them in her lap. She hugged them to her chest, grateful for every smudge and dingy scratch.

Henry had saved her from her mother's wrath, but he avoided Lucy's gaze when she tried to thank him. Boys were so confusing! One minute talkative, and the next...

"He's a moody crow," said Quill, watching her brother return to his seat at the back of the canoe, "but he always helps." She grimaced. "Some people, I wish he would not help."

"You mean..." Lucy began, but then clamped her mouth shut. *You mean the Chief's brother and that scarred man?* She wanted to ask. *The scary scarred man?*

Quill stared at her. Lucy hoped she hadn't spoken out loud. "Did I...?"

"No," said Quill, but one way or another Lucy knew Quill had understood.

Lucy dozed against her father's knees, the afternoon breeze cooling her face. She felt like a raw fish breaded in egg and sand, then fried. She fell asleep, waking when Quill touched her elbow. Lucy's mother waited on the beach in her white dress, with a light blue shawl draped around her shoulders. Surfacing from a deep sleep, Lucy felt as if everything looked unreal. Her mother's figure seemed to flicker in the strong light, and she seemed small and alone with the dark forest behind her.

"Quill," Lucy said, as they were stepping out of the canoe, "Come visit me! I'll read to you!"

Quill nodded. Henry also turned around.

"Soon?" asked Lucy.

"Soon," said her new friend, with a nod.

Lucy found herself hoping she'd seen a slight nod from Henry as well.

That night, Lucy stayed awake long enough to write in her journal. The shells around her neck clinked as she pulled out a letter tucked into the pages. The letter was from Emily, and had been waiting for her on the table at home. Finally! She'd begun to wonder if all her friends had forgotten her.

Dearest Lu,

Have you finally arrived? How's everything?

Are any of the locals handsome?

Here's the news from home: The most divine young lady has moved into your house. Her name's Shelby and her father sells spectacles, and she has a truly annoying little brother, but also a duck, and guess what? She loves to spy just like you did. But she's not nearly as good at it as you. We had the most wonderful tea together in my garden yesterday.

I have to hurry. Father is tapping his heel in the hallway. He's posting some letters of business for the San Francisco mail and promised to take this one, too.

All my love. Write soon please!

Then she'd scrawled a hasty signature. Emily's words made Lucy's chest ache. Replaced already! She was glad the letter hadn't arrived a week before. She might have pitched in her lot and stowed away on the mail-packet boat. But today, she felt a little better about life. She tucked away the letter and slid into a sleep full of waves and wind, with the taste of strawberry lingering in her mouth, the clink of shells in her ears, and her mother a faint smudge on the horizon of dark forest.

CHAPTER 9

Trappers, Scalps, and other Losses

The morning after the canoe trip, both Lucy and her father slept through church. She rushed downstairs, expecting her mother to be pale and irritated. Instead, she found her at the kitchen table holding one of the red berries. She dropped it on her tongue and chewed slowly with her eyes closed. Then she opened them, and smiled at Lucy.

"Quick now, sleepyhead, get changed and do your chores. Someone's coming to call!"

In Boston, they'd entertained a host of guests for tea and dinner. Here, the only visitors they'd received so far were Katherine's father and the sheriff. The room smelled of buttery scones, and there was a sing-song tone in her mother's voice. She'd even pulled her best dress out of the travel chest. Lucy couldn't imagine who might deserve this much fancy.

"Did you know the word fancy comes from *fantasy?* As in inclination, whim or desire?" she asked, remembering a favorite from *Webster's.* "I love that. Fantasy."

Sometimes her mother became quite irritated with Lucy's dreaminess, especially when there were chores to do. Today she laughed, and Lucy wondered if she'd gotten her real mother back—the one from before the bad times. "That is lovely, daughter of mine," she said, "but if you don't get to work, the tea cakes might all disappear before you're done."

Eager to see the visitor arrive, Lucy kept one eye on the front door while doing her chores. But one of the chickens picked a fight with Dodger. Fur was flying and she had to separate them and clean up the mess.

"Come into the front room," her mother called, when Lucy had finally finished. She stopped for a moment to brush the fur and feathers off her dress, feeling woefully un-fancy and very hungry.

Her mother sat with a middle-aged woman. The lady wore a gray shirt that shimmered silver in the light, decorated with a blue cameo pin. But her skirt and everything else was a dull black, which told Lucy that she was in mourning.

"This is Mrs. Ebey-Blanc, dear."

Ebey? As in, Ebey-without-his-scalp? "Ebey?" she squeaked.

Her mother gave Lucy the "Manners please!" look.

"Colonel Ebey was my brother." Blue eyes sized her up and Lucy thought she saw humor there, beneath the gray curls. "Heard something about him, have you?" the lady asked.

"Well, I—"

"Whatever she's heard is of no consequence," said her mother. "Lucy, sit down and fill your mouth with jam tarts, please."

"Call me Mrs. Blanc, please!" the lady said. "My husband insisted I keep both names when we married, like royalty." She smiled, a little sadly. "But it's too much!"

After a few moments of sipping and safe topics, her mother said, "Mrs. Blanc has kindly offered to give you French lessons."

"Fank you!" said Lucy, spitting crumbs out the sides of her mouth.

"Maybe you should give her finishing lessons as well!" said her mother.

Mrs. Blanc smiled. "Your father says you're quite good at conversation." Silver chains glittered when she moved, and she wore a picture locket with a strand of braided hair for a bow. Lucy stared, wondering if it were Colonel Ebey's picture and hair. But how could she have his hair if they'd taken the scalp?

Mrs. Blanc caught her eye. "Lucy, shall we study French together?"

"Mmm?" answered Lucy, trying to hush the clamoring voice in her mind. *Don't think about the scalp. Not the scalp. Not Mr. Ebey. Think about French.*

"Did he... was he... Mr. Ebey... Did they really...?"

"Did he what, dear?" Mrs. Blanc asked.

"Lucy!" her mother's voice jumped to a higher pitch.

"I'd be very happy to study French with you," Lucy said, staring at the locket. Now, this was worth a letter home! Life here had seemed so dull, compared to Boston, but this...

"*Tres bon!*" Mrs. Blanc smiled, and then stood. "I must go. So much to do, always!"

"French lessons!" Her mother twirled Lucy around the porch, then stopped to peer into her face. "What do you think?"

"*Mais oui!*" said Lucy. The French lady next door in Boston had spoken with Lucy every day since she was two, and it would be wonderful to practice again. But then, also truly awful! If you added speaking French to all the other ways she was different.... *Might as well be an albino,* she thought, like the albino rhinoceros she'd read about in *World Atlas of Fanciful Facts.*

Her mother looked happier than she had since they'd arrived, so Lucy tried to drum up some excitement. "Who would have believed it?" she said. "A French teacher, out here in the wilderness?"

Her mother laughed. "This isn't the wilderness." But she smoothed the fabric of her dress and sighed, giving the lie to her words. "Did you know... Mrs. Blanc taught at a fine school for young ladies, in San Francisco?" asked her mother. "That is, until she met Mr. Blanc."

"Tell me," Lucy said, and they sat down on the top step together.

"She met him at a trading post. He was a French trapper out of the mountains, bringing in furs, and she was visiting a friend. She came from a rich family in New Hampshire—in shipping I think. Anyway, they met in the middle of the street and I guess that was that."

Lucy had a hard time imagining the lady with a hairy old trapper. "And?"

"He was smitten! A week later they married and moved here. He traded with the local tribes while she watched over the building of their lovely home."

"What happened to him?" Lucy imagined a war party, or a bear, or...

"He died, sweetheart, in a wreck at sea, carrying a boatload of furs."

"A shipwreck? Poor Mrs. Blanc!"

"It is sad." Her mother surprised her by smiling. "Don't you worry about Mrs. Blanc. She brought your father here, and now she's wanting 'opera and theater acts.'" Her mother shook her head and the sun sparked in her honey-colored hair. "I'd feel sorry for the town council!"

Lucy felt her mother's hand on her forehead, stroking away loose strands of hair as they talked about French, and what to plant next to the Kentucky Blue Wonder string beans in the garden. It had been a long while since she'd touched Lucy's hair that way.

The new week began with a clatter of pans and the smell of fresh bread. For the first time in weeks, Lucy's mother was up early. She was bundling up bread and salt pork when Lucy came down for breakfast. She gave Lucy a quick kiss and handed the food to Lucy's father. "I'm off to the mercantile for thread."

Her father smiled.

"Thread?" asked Lucy, "For what? May I go?"

"Oh, projects," said her mother, evasively, "... and no, of course you may not. School!"

Lucy's mood fell a little. Her quilt was getting quite worn and she'd hoped her mother would make her a new one for the cold nights, or a dress like the ones the other girls wore.

"I'll be late again tonight," said her father. He'd taken on extra work at the port, helping with the customs business. His teaching brought in gifts of fish, furs, and some tobacco twists, but no real money. One resident had even left a jug of moonshine on their porch. Her mother had used it to strip the floors and bleach the kitchen sink.

"Who'll walk me home?" asked Lucy.

"Katherine, of course," said her mother. "I'd like you to bring her in so I can thank her." Her mother looked her in the eye. "I'll be watching for you."

Up until now, Lucy had given a wave toward the path—pretending her escorts were in the woods. She'd wanted to tell her mother that she was walking home alone; but after weeks of lying, it was hard to fess up. Katherine would never walk with Lucy just to keep her from getting in trouble... especially for that reason. Katherine liked trouble the way most people liked candy.

Over and over, Lucy tried to start fresh, and over and over she made the same mistakes. Her first week, Lucy had brought a china doll to school for the small girls. They'd loved it, but Katherine had somehow pushed in. The doll "accidentally" fell and shattered. The same thing had happened with Lucy's magnifying glass and a sewing hoop, both of which were quite cheap but which Katherine called "pricey show-off stuff."

This morning, a package waited for Lucy on her desk. Her instincts told her to hide it, but her father insisted she open it up. As the brown paper fell away, she saw that Mrs. Blanc had gifted her a blue book. The title was engraved in gold leaf on the cover: *The Hunchback of Notre Dame*. The card read, "This is THE sensation in France. Be prepared to read!"

Lucy ran her hands over the smooth cover. She would save it for later, when she was alone. Katherine took the book away and weighed it in her hand. "Little Miss French!" she said, flicking the pages with a dirty thumbnail.

A few minutes before, Lucy had felt brim full of buttery

sunshine. Her mother was better, and she loved French. So she decided not to let Katherine ruin her mood. She took the book back and balanced it on top of her head, saying, "*Oui*, that's me, little Miss French!" Her father rebuked Lucy, but the children looked surprised and delighted. Katherine didn't seem to know what to do, and sat down. Lucy was glad to have gotten the better of her, for once.

At morning break, the children played outside in the dappled light under the oaks, and Lucy tied her handkerchief around the eyes of the littlest one for blind man's bluff. Ruby sidled over and asked her about her weekend. Ruby had never spoken directly with Lucy at school before, not with Katherine around. Katherine seemed to have disappeared, so Lucy took her chance and was pleased to tell Ruby about Quill and her strawberry picking outing.

"Oh, I love strawberries!" said Ruby. Her eyes widened. "But weren't you afraid?"

Lucy read the suggestion in the girl's face. "Of Quill and her family? You've been reading too many *Copper Penny Horror Stories*!"

"Lucky!" said Ruby with a shiver. Just then Katherine sauntered onto the back porch of the school, looking pleased as cream. Ruby hustled away to the other side of the meadow.

Katherine's happy mood made Lucy uneasy, even more so when the girl agreed to walk her home the first time she asked. They made their way through the woods path, with several of the girls meandering behind. Katherine walked right up to Lucy's front door, and even accepted Lucy's mother's invitation to have a cookie, eating three and taking one back to the crowd that huddled at the edge of the woods.

On the walk home, Lucy had heard whispers behind her but ignored them. She'd been so relieved that her mother wouldn't have a reason to check into her afternoons. Maybe now the girls would let her go downtown with them again. As they left, Lucy heard an explosion of laughter from Katherine and murmurs from the others. Ruby looked back, her face troubled.

Watching from the doorway, Lucy's mother said, "She seems nice enough, considering her family background." Katherine turned back at the edge of the woods and Lucy could swear she saw a gleam of malice in her eye, even from that distance.

Lucy nodded at her mother, still feeling the prickle of unease at the back of her neck, and went to visit Dodger, giving him a nice long hop through the meadow grasses. No one should be locked up on such a nice day.

Her mother was in a mood to scrub and tidy, so Lucy hadn't a moment to go up to her room and look at Mrs. Blanc's gift until bedtime. Now she could study the lovely blue cover with its gilded pages and gold lettering. She had trouble with the knot, which looked different than when she'd tied it. When the paper fell away, she knew why Katherine had gloated all afternoon. The spine was broken. Pages had been ripped out, ragged, right from the middle, as well as all the photo plates and their covering tissue. Lucy felt ill. The gold leaf had been scratched from the sides with fingernails... a set of long, dirty fingernails.

CHAPTER 10

A Little Kindness

Lucy kept her head down at school the next morning. Rule number one as the teacher's daughter: Don't ask him to solve your problems with other students. They'll only get worse, and everyone will hate you for tattling. She so wished she could tell her father about the damage to her beautiful book, while he puffed on his pipe and thought of something comforting to say.

The loud voice at the back of the classroom grated on Lucy. Katherine raised her hand to answer questions during lessons, cooperating for the first time ever in school history. Halfway through the day, Lucy's father moved Katherine up from the back corner of the room. Evidently she was his new star student. Lucy could feel her in the seat right behind her, gloating, and she was determined not to show how upset she was.

Lucy hoped to talk to Matthias at recess, but his father came to the schoolhouse early to collect him. Mr. Bishop looked very upset and the class listened shamelessly as he explained to Lucy's father that they'd had a problem with a bull escaping. Matthias seemed troubled as he left, though he stopped by her desk. "Are you quite well, Lucy?" he asked in his attempt at a whisper, a rumble that started deep in his chest.

Everyone looked up from their copy books and several pieces of chalk broke in curious fingers. "Fine... I'm fine," she said, feeling her stomach twist. Lucy wasn't fine at all. She felt a clammy chill in the pit of her stomach. Horrible that someone could be so violent, so hateful to that beautiful book. She hadn't known what to do with it, and had hidden it under her bed. She felt like it needed a decent burial under a tree, or maybe at sea.

Before she realized, Matthias had left, looking hurt as he let the screen door fall shut behind him. She should have responded to him more freely, but that was yet another nail in her coffin. Matthias: Smartest boy in the class, and the only one older than Lucy. Of course Katherine would be sweet on him. You could tell by the way she threw dirt clods at his head when he was outside playing stick ball with the other boys.

Lucy wished she'd at least smiled or thanked him for his concern. Once again, Katherine had leached into Lucy's day and soured everything. Before she knew it, the day was over. She'd gotten nothing done, save gaze at her slate and dream of burial places for the murdered book.

"That's all, students! Fine work today!"

Time to walk home. Lucy simply could not take another step with Katherine, who sweetly offered to accompany her. She tried to think of an excuse.

"Dad, can I help you at the docks?"

He laughed. "No."

The other girls fidgeted outside the door while Katherine used her new attitude on Lucy's father, giving him a sickly-sweet smile. Lucy watched in disbelief as he fell for it, nodding his head and smiling. "Very nice work today, Katherine!"

"Hmmmmph!" Lucy snorted, kicking the floor so hard she stubbed her toe on a nail.

"Lucy, what is wrong with you today? You've been so short-tempered since the moment you got up!" He frowned. "I'm in mind not to let you go to Mrs. Blanc's today."

"Mrs. Blanc's?"

Behind Lucy's father, Katherine made a face.

"Did you listen to a word your mother and I said this morning?" He gathered up his books and propelled her through the door. She thought back and couldn't remember the morning. "Did you bring your book, like your mother asked?"

"What book?"

"You didn't?"

"No, father," she pleaded. "Please."

His voice rose. "I asked you as well. How could you forget?"

Lucy shook her head again, miserable. Few things were taken as seriously in their house as the proper care of books. He gave her his ultimate sign of displeasure, turning his back on her. But he said, "Mrs. Blanc is waiting so you'd best go."

She waited until the girls were out of sight before starting for Mrs. Blanc's house. Well, she thought, at least I don't have to go with the others.

Only ten years before, the Plummer Family had built the first settler cabin in Port Townsend, on the long stretch of beach below the cliff. The Plummer house fit Lucy's image of a pioneer town: a rough cabin on a cold beach. But Mrs. Blanc's house turned that thought on its head. It would have been at home in any town in New England. White with blue trim, it had large bay windows, roses blooming along a picket fence, and a wrap-around porch. Perched on the bluff, it had a commanding view of the straits and Whidbey Island on the opposite side, and the waterfront area below.

Lucy lingered by Mrs. Blanc's fence, remembering other roses in other gardens. Emily had written the day before with all the news—plans for summer with Shelby, and which girls had been casting their eyes after which boys. Could life ever be so sweet here?

"Ready to come in, *mademoiselle*?"

Mrs. Blanc stood on her porch. She wore a dove-gray skirt and a white shirt. The colors told Lucy that Mrs. Blanc's mourning had eased a bit. Her gaze rested on Lucy's face for a moment, as if about to ask her a question. Instead, she led her into a bright room with a globe in the middle and book shelves from floor to ceiling. Light filtered through the bay windows, falling on polished oak floors. Lucy wished she didn't have the book to think about, as she'd normally love this room.

"I had the oak flooring shipped all the way from New Hampshire," said Mrs. Blanc.

"All that way?" Most people used wood from the local mills.

"Sometimes you just want to be a little different."

"Sometimes you are," said Lucy, "even if you don't want to be." She could hear the bitterness in her own voice.

The lady's eyebrows arched. "Time for French," she said. "Lucy, where's your book?"

Lucy turned away to hide the tears that suddenly filled her eyes. What could she say? If she told Mrs. Blanc the truth, she might go to Lucy's father... or even Katherine's! Lucy shuddered at the thought. She'd better not.

Mrs. Blanc cleared her throat. "If you want to tell me, I'm a good listener. Otherwise, let's review vocabulary, shall we?" She made a great production of finding her book, giving Lucy a chance to wipe her eyes. She settled herself at the table, grateful not to be pried open like a shell with a pearl.

"I'm so sorry," said Lucy. "The book was—I mean is—beautiful. I, uh, lost it."

Mrs. Blanc studied her for a long moment, then drilled her on vocabulary. Lucy's French had grown so rusty, her head hurt by the time they decided to take a break. Her teacher said, "Wait here while I get us some tea."

Lucy couldn't resist sitting in the window seat. She'd spent hours in the one at their Boston house—reading, watching the street, or snuggling in for a gossip with friends. Even awful Katherine had Ruby, and Lucy felt an ache when she saw their heads tucked close in conversation.

"It's never easy," said Mrs. Blanc, returning with a laden tray, "to start in a new place." She set it down and passed Lucy a cup of tea, then settled herself in the window seat. "Don't I know! When I first arrived, some of the others looked sideways at me."

"At you? But you're so stylish!"

Mrs. Blanc smiled. "They knew I had an education," she said, and picked up one of the light blue cups rimmed in gold. "I think they were a little embarrassed."

"No one's embarrassed around me!"

"Are you sure?"

Katherine's ripped boots came to mind.

"You're a smart young lady," Mrs. Blanc said, tipping Lucy's chin, "and with those blue eyes of yours, and that hair, I can see another reason for jealousy."

Matthias flew into her head. All the girls had been setting their caps for him for years. Lucy felt too young for him, but the few words Matthias spoke were usually aimed her way.

"What am I to do? Stop talking? Pull out all my hair?" She knew her hair was her best feature.

Mrs. Blanc patted her hand. "You'll be glad not to be bald when you're older dear."

Lucy found herself spilling out the story of the book. Mrs. Blanc nodded, frowned and exclaimed at all the proper points; but she did not interrupt. "I'm sorry to have caused such trouble," she said. "I should have known not to send it to the school."

"Oh no!" said Lucy. "It was such a lovely thing for you to do for me. It's my fault!"

Mrs. Blanc shook her head. "Disturbed... that girl's a problem." She took Lucy's hands. "You need to tell your father."

Lucy pulled her hands away. "No! I can't!"

The lady frowned. Lucy knew adults never understood the inside workings of a school. Mrs. Blanc urged her once again to tell him. "He needs to know, Lucy, as the teacher if not as your father." Then she switched the subject to one Lucy had been dying to hear about.

"You must be curious," said Mrs. Blanc, "... about my brother, Colonel Ebey."

"Am I ever!" Lucy hadn't meant to say that aloud! She groaned and put her hands over her face. "I mean, that is... yes, a little."

Mrs. Blanc didn't seem to be listening. She gazed out the window toward Whidbey Island and shook her head. "Such a horrid night! Isaac went out with a lamp because the dogs were barking crazily. We barely escaped out a back window."

We? Lucy felt a chill pass over her. "You were there?"

"Oh yes," Mrs. Blanc nodded. "People were rushing about outside, and we didn't know what was happening. We hid in the trees all night, afraid to make a noise—Isaac's wife and daughters and I."

"At dawn, my poor brother—Winfield—found him." Her voice dropped. "He wouldn't let any of us see." Lucy tried not to imagine, but all sorts of gruesome images assembled in her mind. She was glad Ruby wasn't present to give them living color.

"But..." she ventured to say, "who did it?"

Mrs. Blanc looked at her in surprise. "Now that is the question, indeed. When my husband was still alive he traded with many tribes."

Lucy gave her an encouraging nod.

"He said it was a group in a large canoe, from very far away."

"But why?"

"Most claim it was random violence, and some use Isaac as an excuse to push the local tribes onto reservations." She thought for a moment. "I think it was all a terrible mistake. They wanted someone else."

They drank their tea in silence for a while.

Mrs. Blanc continued. "Lucy, children say—well, *things*. What else have you heard that you're not telling me?"

Normally, Lucy wouldn't answer directly. Her mother had made perfectly clear what was and wasn't to be said. But the lady regarded her with a calm curiosity that put Lucy at ease. "They say his ghost wanders the beach over there, looking," she blurted out.

"For what?"

"For... his head," Lucy said reluctantly.

Mrs. Blanc surprised Lucy by laughing. "Children! There was a girl in my grade school —Lenora Hedgely was her name—told us her grandpa's ghost lurked in the attic. We stayed up all night hoping to see him, but no ghost. I think the girl had bad digestion."

She became serious. "Don't believe every tale you hear. My brother lies peacefully in his grave." She set her hands in her lap, one on top of the other. "I'm dreadfully sad he's gone, but he was a good man and has no reason to walk the nights and scare small children."

Lucy knew for a fact that not all of him was at rest, with the scalp in possession of the Indians who had killed him. She'd read that efforts were being made to recover it, but she managed to keep this to herself. "What happened to his widow and children?"

Mrs. Blanc shook her head. "Still there, on the island." She pointed through her front window at a green valley, across the water on Whidbey's Island. "That white house, the one up from the beach."

They went out on the porch to look. The house was large enough to be visible across the water, and sat in a green field above the beach. Cliffs rose at either end of the broad valley.

"That's her house. You'll see it advertised in *The Register*. They call it the *Ferry House* because people stop on their way to the ferry." Lucy heard something in Mrs. Blanc's voice. "It's made from the boards of Isaac's original cabin, which was pulled down. She'll never recover fully... never be the same." From the little she knew of Mrs. Blanc, Lucy couldn't imagine her being permanently undone by anything. For herself, Lucy had to admit the episode was unsettling. Poor Mrs. Ebey.

Lucy's father knocked at the door and she jumped. She'd enjoyed her afternoon, but she found herself wanting the comforts of home.

No one walked Lucy home from school for the rest of the week. Her mother kept looking at her, as though about to ask her a question. After three days of Katherine gloating and mouthing the word, *book*, Lucy couldn't face one more day. On Friday she pretended to be sick, and her mother let her stay home without an argument.

CHAPTER 11

Learning Letters, Reading Signs

Saturday morning, Lucy found her mother bent over the table, holding her side. Lucy insisted she go back to bed, and then lit the fire and baked the day's bread. She opened the door to fetch water and found Quill perched in the middle of the front step.

"Quill!"

"Did you remember?" asked the girl.

"Oh, of course!" said Lucy, putting down her pail and wondering how long she'd been sitting there. "Wait here."

She intended to do much more than simply read to Quill. *If father won't invite Quill to school*, she thought as she pillaged her father's supplies, *I'll just have to bring school to Quill*. She dug out a primer and slate, some chalk, and a *McGuffey's Reader*.

When Lucy handed Quill the *McGuffey's Reader*, she held it like it was made of solid gold. Lucy watched as she ran her fingers along the cover, the binding, and down the side of the rough cut pages. A reader wasn't exactly a fine specimen, but Quill's face glowed. Lucy couldn't help contrasting her treatment of the book with what Katherine had done. Lucy dropped down next to Quill on the step, casting glances to each side to see if Henry might be lurking somewhere nearby, but Quill was alone. Lucy felt a little dampened.

"We start with the alphabet." She formed a large *A* and a little *a* on the slate. "Here, copy this." She pushed the slate toward Quill. The girl looked startled, but she leaned over the slate and started to copy, holding the chalk all cramped up in her hand.

"No, no!" said Lucy, taking Quill's fingers and pressing the thumb and first finger into a proper grip. The chalk broke.

"You're too serious!" Lucy laughed. "Ease yourself a little!" She wiggled Quill's elbows the way her piano teacher used to do and Quill leaned over the slate again, intent. One strand of dark hair fell against the girl's cheek as she carefully formed the letters, then held the slate out.

"Good!" said Lucy. The lines were a little quavery, but perfectly respectable. "A" she pronounced, "is for apple."

"A is for apple," said Quill, forming the word in her mouth as though she were saying something completely foreign.

Lucy looked around. What could be more elementary than an apple? But then she realized Quill might not have seen an apple before. The saplings they'd brought were little more than sticks in the ground. "Wait!" she said. "You!"

"You," Quill repeated dutifully. "A is for you." She looked confused, mouthing the *ya* sound at the beginning of *you* and looking at the A on her slate.

"No, no, no!" said Lucy. "Y is for you. A is for apple."

The girl repeated, "A is for Apple." She looked confused. "A is for me?"

"No, not A," Lucy said. She took the slate and wrote a big Q. "Q is for you, Quill. But also quill pen." She held up the quill pen she'd been using to write the letters on a piece of scrap paper for Quill to take with her. But that's the opposite end of the alphabet and we are at the beginning." She thought for a moment, then turned the page and pointed. "Q is for Quail!"

Quill copied the Q, adding a flourish to the circle and smiling. "The letter has a tail too, like the bird." Then she turned to Lucy. "And you?" she asked.

"No, no!" said Lucy. Teaching was hard work. "Y is for you."

"No, no!" mimicked Quill, shaking her head. "What letter for *you*?" She poked Lucy in the chest.

"For me? L is for me, Lucy." She took the chalk and wrote an L on the slate. Quill copied it, forming the L in her mouth.

"But what is for you?" Quill asked. "I'm Quill and small q quill, and quail with a tail." She wagged her bottom and pointed to the alphabet page, then pointed at Lucy.

They turned back to the L page and found that L was for lark. Lucy described the bird and its song, feeling sure there were none in the Washington Territory. "Larks sing. It's lovely." She sighed and pointed to her leg. "Not as pretty, but L is also for leg."

"L is for leg." Quill covered her mouth and Lucy realized she was smirking under her hand. "What?" she asked, "Tell me!"

"L is for leg and Lucy...because you wander on your legs." She made the sign for walking with her two fingers. "And you get in trouble for it!" She tipped her head sideways and said, "What's the letter for trouble?"

Lucy formed the letter T on the slate Quill was holding. "Then, T is for Henry!" Quill said. Lucy agreed and they both laughed. "But H is actually for Henry." She showed Quill how to write both Quill and Henry on the slate, feeling taxed by the way Quill's curiosity romped through letters and subjects. She was soaking up letters like parched soil with a rainfall.

The girls worked a long time, stopping only when Lucy's mother brought out biscuits and blackberry juice. She patted Lucy's head briefly as she walked by, but did not interrupt them. Lucy watched her mother's slow progress up the steps, and how softly she closed the screen door. They made it through all the capitals and smalls to H before Lucy noticed the bucket still sitting on the porch.

"I need to help my mother."

"I will help also," said Quill. "I help the mothers in our house." She paused, "Can we learn more after?"

Quill's quest to read might just wear Lucy out. "I don't know," Lucy said. Inside, her mother was trying to lift the kettle to start the wash.

"Oh, I understand," said Quill, and followed Lucy into the house. But she looked disappointed.

Lucy took the kettle from her mother, and they pulled her over to a chair. Quill put two pillows behind her and motioned for Lucy to prop her feet up. Lucy's mother closed her eyes and leaned her head back on the pillow, with the breeze from the open window fanning her pale cheeks. She sighed.

Lucy rolled up her sleeves and lit a fire under the boiling pot in the yard. She grabbed the big bucket, then she and Quill started the parade from pump to pot, taking turns at the pump. Lucy was in her element now. After stirring up the fire and adding lye to the water, they boiled the clothes.

The day had blossomed into a truly lovely late-June blessing, but the girls had little time to enjoy it. "Is Henry near here?" Lucy asked, looking toward the surrounding forest.

Quill shook her head and pressed her lips together, and Lucy wondered where he was.

The clothes swirled by in the water: Lucy's petticoats, her father's handkerchiefs and collars, her mother's aprons and summer stockings, and unmentionables. Quill lifted up various pieces saying, "What's this?"

Lucy frowned, thinking about underthings and how to explain her mother's. She was sure Quill's aunties didn't have anything so uncomfortable beneath their dresses, with all the snaps and hooks. Then the obvious clonked her in the head so hard she was speechless. She thunked her forehead with the heel of her hand.

Quill stood with the paddle in her hand, dangling a ladies' petticoat. "What?"

"My mother!"

"Yes?" Quill nodded, as if agreeing to something Lucy hadn't yet said. "She doesn't look well."

Flushing, Lucy said. "I'm sure now...she's expecting a baby!"

Quill rolled her eyes. "Well, yes. I knew since I first saw her."

A flash of irritation passed as Lucy felt the relief of knowing for sure. "I should have noticed before: she's not been using her monthly cloths. I'd know, because I do all the laundry now. I guess I didn't think about it when we were on the ship." Lucy wondered how women dealt with the irritating facts of female life in the tribe, but felt much too embarrassed to ask.

"Will you tell me?" Quill asked. She stared down into the pot at the swirling clothes.

"What?"

"Why you are so worried about this?" Quill shrugged. "Everyone has babies."

Lucy took over the stirring, but she didn't answer. The girls had soaped, scrubbed, wrung, and were hanging the things out to dry when Quill spoke again. "When did you mother stop having her moon time?"

"What?" asked Lucy, "Oh...I don't know. I haven't even been thinking about that, only how much laundry I had to finish." Lucy's own body was still that of a girl. Looking sideways at Quill, she spied the outlines of a more developed figure under the old dress, and guessed that Quill had already crossed that first line into womanhood.

"A new child," said Quill with a smile. "That is good! Your house has very few people."

"NOT good!" said Lucy, "Not good at all!"

Quill laid a hand on Lucy's arm to stop her washing. "Tell me. Why?"

Under Quill's brown-eyed gaze the whole story came out. "You must wonder why there's only me? Everyone else does!" said Lucy. "My mother had two babies after me. Both of them died before a week was out, and my mother almost died too." Lucy realized she was almost yelling and lowered her voice. "There was blood everywhere, then. I saw it in the laundry." Quill was the first person in a long time Lucy had told about those two small ones who lay in the ground back at the Boston Cemetery. She knew her mother had gone to see them, a few days before they set sail.

Over the years, Lucy had guessed several times that her mother might be carrying another small bump. But they had passed each time with blood, a lot of blood.

Quill nodded and sighed. "We lose many babies too, especially in winter."

Lucy wanted to ask, *And mothers? Do you lose mothers too?*

Frowning, Quill said, "Of course we do. Too many."

"Oh no, I didn't mean to say that to you. I was only wondering, in here." She pointed to her head, then her mouth. "Unfortunately, I don't know when I've whispered it here."

Quill moved to the clothes line and carefully folded a sheet, pressing the creases as she folded it over each time. Then she looked Lucy in the eye. "It's all right," she said. "...to talk about such things."

"We don't," said Lucy shortly. Quill simply nodded.

"Mother, are you feeling all right?" Lucy asked that night. Quill had finally gone home after helping Lucy peg out the laundry to dry. When she came inside, she'd caught her mother at the sink, washing out cloths. The water looked red, before her mother stepped in and pulled the drain plug.

"Yes," she said, "I'm fine." She turned and scrubbed at an invisible spot in the sink. They'd never spoken about her mother's *trouble*. Lucy opened her mouth.

"Lucy," warned her father, from the corner of the room.

Her mother creased and re-creased the cloth towel on the drain board, exactly the same way Quill had creased the sheet earlier in the day. She wondered what men did when they wanted to avoid answering a question. Her father puffed mightily on his pipe, creating a cloud of smoke.

Lucy found herself wishing for a big family, like Quill's, so there wouldn't be so much silence. She fled the room and went to pull feathers from the rooster's tail to send with her next letter. Emily knew about babies. So did June, and even Katherine. Well, now her house would have a baby too, if everything went all right. *And if not?* A little voice asked inside her head.

She sat in the coop for a long time with a chicken on her lap. She'd spent a lot of time there since they'd arrived. A nice warm chicken helped a person think.

Had her mother lost another baby today? Surely there wasn't enough blood for that?

That night, the clouds returned and the wind blew off Point Wilson. The eaves creaked and the whole house shook, and Lucy's bedroom seemed a long way from her parents' on the main floor. Her arms were weary and her back ached, and her tired brain boiled with questions. She spirited Dodger up to her room. He was tame and fat, and his fuzzy bulk stretched against her helped her relax and fall sleep. But her dreams were haunted. She searched through thick trees and darkness for her mother's voice, which grew faint as Lucy clawed through branches and undergrowth. Quill and Mrs. Blanc appeared and disappeared, looking concerned, as did her father; but they seemed unable to help, or even speak.

This is ridiculous, Lucy thought, the next morning. One way or another, I need to know.

"Lucy," her father said, in his extra calm voice. "Your mother's not feeling well."

"Because of the baby?" she blurted out.

Both her parents' mouths gaped open. They looked at each other, and her father sat down.

"Why didn't you tell me?" she asked.

"We didn't want to disappoint you if... "

"If the baby died," said Lucy. The words fell like lead into the air. She expected to see the tight look cross her mother's face; but today her mother seemed different. She'd been up early, and set a nice breakfast for Lucy's last day of school before Summer Vacation.

"Lucy," warned her father.

"This child won't die," said her mother calmly. "I had a few pains yesterday, but everything seems to be fine today."

"We need to make sure your mother doesn't work too hard," said her father. "Doctor's orders!" His voice was light, but his face told a different story.

CHAPTER 12

Summer!

Freedom, finally! Summer vacation had arrived and Quill visited often, learning to sound out the alphabet and her first words. She insisted on helping Lucy with her chores to pay for her lessons, and Lucy didn't mind the company or the extra set of hands.

Temperatures went up and the grasses dried in every open space around town. Beans swelled on the vines, and the air smelled of wildflowers. One hot morning, Lucy heard a whirring sound next to her ear while she was picking beans. She turned to see a tiny hummingbird with a coppery red head. It was so close, its wings made a breeze on her cheeks. Out of the corner of her eye, she spied Henry. He was fixing an arrow to his bowstring.

"Don't!" Lucy cried, and the bird fled with a buzz of its wings.

"Too small," said Henry, shrugging.

Lucy decided on the spot that he was plain, pure boy, like all the others in town. The arrow dwarfed the bird, and Henry must have done it to annoy her.

"Are you here to study?" she asked.

"He is here for your father," said Quill, coming up from behind him.

"Not home at present," said Lucy. "Wait there." She pointed to the steps.

Henry ignored her and propped himself against a tree, pretending not to watch as they began their lesson. They'd reached the three-letter words in *McGuffey's*, but for some reason Quill went all the way back to capital A and small a—humming to herself as she wrote. Lucy started to protest, but Quill winked at her.

Henry moved closer and closer, leaning on his bow and trying to get a glimpse of his sister's writing; but the closer he got, the farther Quill leaned away. Suddenly the bow flexed and Henry fell, sprawled at their feet. He jumped up and brushed himself off with an angry flush, and Quill muttered, "Hothead."

When Lucy's father arrived from town he checked on her mother, who had not regained her color since the day Lucy found her leaning against the table. Quill kept telling Lucy that her mother looked normal, but nothing seemed to touch the unease that flowed like a slippery current underneath every other thought or activity.

The girls convinced Lucy's father to take them along on one of his gathering expeditions for the judge. Evidently Henry had become his local guide. The distrust Lucy had detected in Henry early on had melted away. Now, the two of them moved along the trail together— pointing and talking, breaking off leaves and berries and holding them up to the light.

What a contrast with Katherine. She'd been marching around town the day before with a storm on her face and her body hunched up against the wind. While Lucy was watching from the other side of the street, Katherine had curled her lip at the young girls behind her, as though wanting to be rid of them. It was hard to believe the rumor that Katherine could be very tender with her brothers and sisters.

Quill and Lucy squished themselves into the middle of the canoe and her father and Quill's brother took opposite ends.

"Is Henry learning the alphabet?" whispered Lucy once they were under way.

"Yes!" said Quill, with an impish smile. "But don't ask him about it! At night, I leave your pieces of paper on his mat and say the letters while he looks at them. I pretend I'm just practicing for myself."

"That's a lot of fuss! Why doesn't he come study with us?"

She raised an eyebrow, "Do your boys let girls teach them things?"

"Truthfully? No," answered Lucy. "At least, not unless they're forced to. Boys who spend too much time with girls are called sissies," she admitted.

Quill nodded in agreement. "My uncle George, he tells Henry not to stay with women or do women's work." She made a face. "He says, 'Books are women's work.' But my uncle Chetzmoka, the chief—" Quill paused, as though unsure if she should continue.

"Yes?"

"Well, *he* says we must learn the settler's ways now. Chetzmoka has... " She said a word in S'Klallam. "He worries for us. He wants everyone to get along—be happy." She sighed.

Lucy sighed too. Seeing how little the tribe had left of the whole area that had once been theirs, she thought they wouldn't be allowed to live by their old ways for much longer. She tried to think of a way to help. "You need your own slate!"

"Eh?" said Henry and Quill at the same time.

"A slate!" said Lucy, to both of them. "To practice writing— it's an important skill. We can buy one. I have some coins saved!"

Quill stiffened. "That is your money," she said. Then she pointed at the grassy hills they'd been passing as they hugged the coastline. "I make baskets out of grasses—I learned a new way." Her face brightened. "I can sell them, to your father and maybe the judge?"

Lucy didn't know how many baskets the Smithsonian needed, but they decided that Quill would weave, and she and Lucy would sell them in town to raise money for school supplies. For now, she would enjoy the sunny day: the swallows bombarding the water, and the way the wind rippled across the nearby hills. But Quill had other thoughts on her mind.

"They took my mother on a sunny day," Quill said, with no preamble. "Wickedly cold, but blue skies and sunny." Lucy waited, having learned that Quill spoke best when given room.

"We were at our winter houses," Quill said, "at the bay the settlers call 'Clallam,' after us. Most of the village had gone away to a potlatch, but my mother stayed with the old aunties." Quill hugged her knees. "She was a healer, good with bark and roots, and the elk grease my father brought from the mountains for the old ones' bones." A note of pride warmed Quill's voice that Lucy hadn't heard before.

"I had only a few winters, and my little sister... so small." Quill's eyes went unfocused, and her voice sounded like it came from far away. "When Mother went down to the water; they were hidden in the trees."

"Who?"

"Men from the Island, the one you call Vancouver's." She pointed toward the north.

"White men?"

She shook her head. "No. A tribe from the middle part of that island."

"The same that...you know, Mr. Ebey?" Lucy asked.

Quill shook her head. "No, not so far away. These warriors took her and my small sister. She was still on my mother's back, only a few moons old."

"Didn't anyone do anything?"

"The old aunties heard her scream for help, but could not get there fast enough. They watched the paths of the canoes fade in the water after them, as the moon rose, a most beautiful moon, they say." She paused. "Warriors went out with my father when they came from the potlatch a few days later," Quill said, "but it was too late."

Lucy had assumed Quill's mother was dead from illness, like the many Indians who died of the pox when traders first came; or that she'd died birthing a child. But this...to have her stolen away. "Do you think she's still alive?"

"If so, she is a slave," said Quill, "or a chief took her as second wife, maybe...."

"Yes?"

Quill shook her head, picking at a stray thread in her skirt. "I do not look to see her again, or my sister."

A hundred questions boiled in Lucy's mind. How could you have a mother alive somewhere and not try to find her? How could you take a mother from her children or have slaves? But then she remembered the terrible war raging on the other side of the country, between the North and South, over slaves. She opened her mouth to ask, but Quill's face folded closed like the pages of a book.

They still had a stretch of water to cover, and the girls were sick of hearing about fish and spears. Lucy decided to read from *The Hunchback of Notre Dame*. It seemed that Judge Swan was a Victor Hugo fan, and he'd offered his copy to her. She had a feeling that Mrs. Blanc was behind the offer.

For Lucy, there was nothing like a new book—the clean smell of it, the feel of the paper, the sound of the knife slicing through folded pages. She couldn't believe they hadn't been cut open yet! The judge had been so kind to loan it to her new.

The book was in French, like the one Katherine had destroyed. Lucy did her best to translate, with everyone helping. Words were tossed back and forth in a salad of three languages. Her father didn't speak any French, Henry spoke little English, and only the twins spoke Clallam. But the story was strong, and the picture plates helped show the scenes.

After awhile the others fell silent, and Lucy read on. It felt as if the moment might go on forever, with her father dreaming in the bow, a smile playing around Henry's lips, and Quill's eyes alight. She had a powerful memory, and Lucy wondered if she was memorizing the story so she could retell it later.

Henry beached the canoe on the opposite side of Discovery Bay from a mill. Lucy was about to step out into the shallow water, as she usually did, when she realized Henry had turned back and stood with his hand extended toward her. He held her arm for only a moment, but the strength of his grip supported her over the tipsy bow onto dry sand until her feet were steady, though her heart seemed to stumble a little in its beat.

As he ran to catch up to her father, Lucy traced patterns in the sand with her boot and considered the nature of a true gentleman.

Quill had tired of waiting. "Lucy! A little more quickly?"

"You sound like my mother," Lucy said under her breath.

The air was alive with the sounds of a nearby stream, and her father had stopped to collect a tiny nest. "Hummingbird!" he pointed at one of the green and scarlet birds aiming its beak at him. It was identical to the one that Henry had pretended to shoot.

"You can't take her nest!" Lucy protested.

"That's a he," said her father. "Only the males have that scarlet head and neck. If you won't let me collect the nest, will you make a sketch?" He thrust his drawing pad at her, and he and Henry moved off up the stream.

Lucy didn't usually do the scientific-type of drawing her father needed, but she did like to sketch. She took up her father's pencil and soon became fascinated with the nest. She worked to place every piece of grass and the tiny, speckled eggs, thinking about the buzzing things that would hatch out and fill the air with whirling wings, like tiny dragons. Quill stood behind her, offering her opinion freely, until Lucy shooed her away.

By the time Lucy caught up to the others, Henry had lifted a pole from his pack. Lucy tried not to stare at the smooth skin rippling on his bare back, or his muscular legs where he'd rolled up his pants to the knee. Down in the water, a fish with hooked jaws thrashed in a square-sided trap. Quill opened the trap gate, and the water frothed as her brother used skill to land the fish as it flipped its powerful body back and forth. Henry tossed it up onto the bank, where it flopped and gasped. He set about the task of killing and preparing the fish with careful, quiet movements.

"This first trap," he said, "catches the biggest fish."

"It belongs to the chief," said Quill.

Her father said, "It's a weir! I've always wanted to see one of these." He gave Lucy the *pay attention* look. She tried to, but he was asking endless questions. Quill seemed restless and wandered away. Lucy followed her to a berry thicket under the trees.

"These ripen when the great ones return each year," Quill said.

"The great ones?" Lucy asked, imagining chiefs and their wives arriving in canoes.

"Salmon," Quill said, and handed a golden berry to Lucy. "Salmonberry."

They stood next to the brown water, which rippled and gurgled. The shade was cool, and they could talk easily while they picked. Quill told Lucy the berries looked like salmon eggs. Lucy thought of her mother, who was swelling like a golden fruit and glowed from within. She took a moment to sketch a branch. Quill glowed when she was reading, and Henry when he played with a seal or paddled over the water, and her father when he was drawing a bird's wing. Lucy wondered what made her golden, filled with light.

"These are my favorite days in the circle of the year. This is my place," said Quill, looking around. "We call a place of shelter like this a 'cradle in the waves,' for the baby who was carried in her bark cradle over the waves. Whole villages died and emptied with the sickness brought by the white man's ships. The baby's village wasted away. No one knows who put her in the cradle, but the waves kept her. They carried her gently, to a new village."

Like Moses in Egypt, thought Lucy.

Quill turned and asked, "Where is your place?"

The question pierced Lucy. She had no answer and laughed a little, startled.

"You must find a place," said her friend, gazing up at the hills behind them, "even as I lose mine."

CHAPTER 13

Trouble Follows

Walking back to the canoe, Quill tried again. "It can be with a person... if you don't like a place." Lucy knew she meant the whole area. She realized that she didn't hate it any more, but she didn't love every pleat in the hills and every bend in the shore the way Quill and Henry did.

"You must find a place with the people in town," said Quill.

"But they hate me!"

"Katherine, yes." Quill shrugged. "Are there no others?"

Lucy shook her head stubbornly.

"Maybe you don't want to see them," said Quill, and walked away.

Anger flashed in Lucy. How dare Quill preach to her! What did she know of being shut in a schoolhouse with Katherine day after day? And how could she lecture Lucy when she didn't seem to have any friends of her own?

Dragging along, Lucy found herself alone in the tall grass near the hummingbird nest. Suddenly, Henry pulled her behind a bush, clamping a hand over her mouth. He pointed at the water. A loud laugh reached her from two white men passing by in a rowboat.

"What's this?" one called out, seeing their small canoe, "Squaws picking berries?" Their laughter made Lucy's stomach feel sick. She could see a whiskey bottle in the nearest one's hand and their clothes looked dirty.

"Let's see if we can scare up some fun, eh?" said one of them, floundering through the water to pull the boat up next to the canoe.

Lucy spotted her father behind a tall clump of grasses, but not Quill. The men were stomping like bulls through the reeds when Lucy spied her. Quill had tripped and was laid out on her side. The basket and the berries she'd picked for Lucy's mother had spilled in front of her, like so much gold on the ground.

The men broke through the reeds and looked down at Quill.

"Ahhhhh," said the first, "I was afraid it was an old, toothless squaw." He moved toward Quill. "What's your name, darlin'?" He reached out a dirty hand toward her long black hair.

Henry released Lucy, and with a jerk he threw something. A whoosh was followed by a scream from the man reaching for Quill's ankle. Henry's knife hit his hand and gashed it, then bounced off to land on the ground. The man held up his bloody hand and looked at it, as though not understanding what had just happened. Before anyone could speak, Lucy's father stepped into the open just as the other man yanked a gun from his sack.

"You see that? He tried to kill me!" the first one howled, rolling his hand in a rag.

"I don't think so," said her father. "Come here Lucy," he continued in his firmest teacher voice. Lucy didn't want to put herself in the gun's path but when she stepped into view, the men grew sheepish.

"Didn't mean no harm," said the first, winking at her father. "Just havin' ourselves a little fun. Rowed over from the mill." He pointed at the building on the other side of Discovery Bay.

"Fun!" her father ground the word between his teeth. "Have it elsewhere, then." He motioned for Lucy and Quill to get into the canoe. Lucy wasn't thinking clearly and tried to pick up the berries. Her father shook his head and said, "Get. In. The. Boat." Quill's ankle had twisted, so Lucy supported her weight as they moved toward the canoe.

Henry had been standing taut as a bow string. Lucy's father motioned for him to get in as well, all the while trying to soothe the men with his words. "We are on an outing together. A pleasant one, fishing. I'm the new teacher in these parts, name's James."

The men protested when Henry stepped toward the canoe. "You lettin' him go?" asked the wounded man. The other jerked his gun toward Henry, and both of them closed in on him.

"You don't want to meet the judge today," said her father, putting himself between the men and Henry.

"The Judge?" said the first. "No justice gonna stir hisself over an Indian!"

Lucy's father planted a hand on Henry, who was coiling himself as though ready to spring.

"Judge Swan would," said her father. "He's a personal friend of mine, and of this boy's family." He pushed Henry into the canoe and shoved off. Lucy noticed that Henry was shaking—though with anger or fear, she wasn't sure. Her father kept a grip on him.

"Swan?" The men laughed, gripping their bellies. "We've seen him holding court... down at the saloon!" They looked unhappy as the canoe drifted away, but they didn't dare shoot now that Lucy and her father were in the boat. At least, Lucy hoped they wouldn't.

When her father had paddled far out into the bay, Lucy started trembling and Quill blazed out at her brother in Clallam. He looked pale; Quill looked paler.

"Put your shirt on, son," said her father and they all stared at Henry's goose-pimpled skin.

Lucy's father followed the other boat with his eyes as the men rowed back toward the Discovery mill. "I hope that's as far as this goes."

Lucy wrote in her journal that night, after looking back over the entries. Her first excitement, *I met an Indian, twin Indians!* And one she'd forgotten, *Matthias is sure nice, and intelligent. I wonder if he notices me?* She propped up the sketch of the hummingbird nest with its tiny eggs on her desk, and wrote the words as they fled through her mind, trying to pin them down. *Today: Bird, berries, basket, knife, gun.* And another thought, surprisingly: *A hand under my elbow.*

CHAPTER 14

Tense in Town, Tense at Home

You need some fresh air," said her mother, handing Lucy a bundle. "Take this supper down to your father."

Had her mother noticed how fidgety Lucy was this morning? Her father had strictly warned her not to mention the incident with the knife to anyone, especially her mother. She felt ready to burst with the details, but had no one to share them with. Maybe a letter? But to whom? Emily's last had been all about Shelby:

What fun we've been having! Throwing water down on all those stuffy girls, walking around like they're queens with their hair pinned up. We got Pearl's older sister yesterday, and Oh My! She was mad. Mother says I may not go out on the balcony for a month.

After what had happened by the Discovery Mill, water games and hair pins seemed a little, well, childish. Port Townsend felt so much more dangerous today as she recalled the gun in the millworker's hand. Then her mind leapt to the Indian in the woods with the scarred arm and the clinking sack. Now her mother wanted her to go through the woods alone? Lucy felt her eyes widen. Now that she could, she wasn't sure she wanted to.

"Do I have to?"

"Honestly, child, I thought you'd been itching to go by yourself?"

Lucy sighed and picked up her father's supper.

"Don't dawdle along the way!" Her mother called from the porch, as Lucy stepped into the trees. She waited a moment, but heard no clinking or footsteps. She hurried along as quietly as possible, and didn't slow down until she'd broken out of the woods and reached the houses of uptown. She came to an abrupt halt. If she tore through town like she was being chased, someone might get the mistaken idea that she was afraid.

Children were out playing in many of the yards and she drew herself up tall, proud to be about town on her own, finally. Lucy paused at the top of the stairs to the waterfront, enjoying the sun on her face. The *Panama* was still in port from San Francisco, though the mail had been delivered days ago. Sailors hurried on and off the ship with casks and bundles on their backs, loading the hold for the return journey. The book under her bed had come from that hold, such a short time ago. Lucy sighed and surveyed the scene.

A few weeks before she would have said the harbor looked positively puny, compared to Boston, but you had to admit Port Townsend was busy: port of call and customs station for the whole territory. You wouldn't find a proper milliner's for your hats, or an ice cream parlor for your sweet tooth, but you would find everything related to ships and cargo—especially at *The Kentucky Store* where they sold everything from shoes to anchors! She knew now that the farmers and their ladies mostly went to Mr. Cady's or the pharmacy. Sailors and miners frequented the hotels, or loitered around the docks. The main thing they had in common seemed to be the saloons.

One thing she had to give the place: its spot on a corner jutting into the ocean made for quite a sight with the water in all its colors of foamy white and green, or steely gray, and the ships skimming along in front of the wind with their sails spread wide and white like wings, or furled in tight against a storm. On a day like this, even the island across the way looked gentle—with the fields Isaac Ebey had cultivated rolling down to the water, lush and green.

At the post office, men were standing at all angles around the place. One was reading *The Port Townsend Register*. Lucy expected to see *Extra! Man Stabbed by Indian boy!* but the news was quite ordinary. On the back of the paper, she read an advertisement for the newest kerosene lamp and one for acrobats coming to the Masonic Lodge. She grinned, thinking that Mrs. Blanc had gotten her way and started the flow of "cultural acts." Before they knew it, she'd order up a full opera, in French!

The man folded the paper, and Lucy's stomach lurched. *Colonel Ebey's Scalp Recovered*, the headline read. Lucy knew she should look away, but she couldn't help reading about how they got his scalp back from the Kake tribe up north. She was leaning in closer to get the particulars of the scalp, and how his hair was still recognizable, when the man looked over the top of his paper and snapped it shut. "You don't want to be looking at THAT, Miss Lucy."

"Oh! You know my name?"

The man smiled at her. "Of course I do! We're not quite the size of New York...yet."

She found herself smiling as she walked down the hall. Lucy poked her head into the office at the back, where her father and Judge Swan were craning over a stack of ledgers. They'd loosed their shirt collars and were talking quietly. She thought she heard something about "Henry," and "witness," and "protect," but they fell silent. Both men looked concerned.

"Miss Lucy!" said the judge, standing to take her hand as though he were greeting a fine lady. He wore a nice suit (though a little rumpled) and a starched white shirt with gold cufflinks. On his desk were a silver pen, an ink bottle, and a journal of green leather etched in gilt with the date: 1862. Heavy leather-bound books filled the shelves on all the walls.

"I hear you're becoming quite a naturalist," he said. "Salmon traps and fresh berries! Wish I'd been invited on one of your outings!"

"Well..." said Lucy doubtfully, thinking of how the day before had ended.

The judge pointed to the little basket Quill had given her father. Quill had not spoken the entire way home from Discovery Bay. Lucy had watched Quill's hands as she wove, pulling and twisting grass into a sweet little cup. She'd given it to Lucy's father when they'd parted.

"Amazing what their weavers can do with grass and a few twigs," said the judge, turning the basket in his hands with a look of wonder on his face. "This is a fine example."

"You're not selling it to the Smithsonian, are you?" she turned to her father.

"Why ever not?" he asked. "We've new expenses coming."

"But Quill made it for *you*," she insisted, and noticed that the judge was listening closely, not laughing or winking the way some adults might have.

"It's an unusual piece," said her father, pointing at the complicated patterns Quill had worked into the strands. "Quill's art will be seen for years to come. She's a gifted weaver."

"Lucy," said the judge, "if someone gives freely, it's yours to keep or give away, don't you think?" He raised an eyebrow.

"Yes, but—"

"She gave it to your father with no conditions on how it was to be used, yes?"

"I guess so," Lucy said, struggling to explain, "but it doesn't *feel* right. That gift was from her to us, to show we're friends, not for business or trading."

She didn't think she'd persuaded anyone, but when her father came home late that night, he left the basket on the table, with a blue eggshell inside.

Lucy heard her parents whispering a few days after the knife incident. She knew by their hushed tones that it related to her, so she crept down the stairs and peeked out.

"Do you think she should?" her mother nodded her head toward the porch, where Quill would soon appear for her lesson.

"Let them be," said her father, "for what little time they have."

"For how long, James?" asked her mother.

Her father's shoe tapped on the floor. "Maybe you're right," he said, and turned toward where Lucy was hiding, raising his voice. "Since you're listening, I might as well tell you directly. You're not to go about with the twins for awhile."

"But... " protested Lucy, coming out of the stairwell. She'd go crazy without the twins' company. "What about Quill's lessons?" Her father frowned at her, but Lucy knew this was the best card to play. "She's getting close to reading on her own!"

Lighting up, he said, "Really? You've come that far with your lessons?"

Now Lucy's mother was frowning.

After regarding her for a moment, her father said, "All right! You can meet here, but don't go anywhere with them." He gazed over her head toward the town, and then spoke. "People are afraid. They feel outnumbered by the Indians."

Lucy thought of Quill's village, surrounded by settler farms and businesses. "That doesn't make any sense! There are so few now."

He lifted up his hand. "The Ebey incident is in everyone's minds now that the scalp is back, hair and all." He frowned. "Some are looking for a reason to push them onto the reservation for good."

"I—I see," Lucy stammered. "But, Discovery Bay... that wasn't Henry's fault!"

"Well, he didn't have to throw the knife."

"They pulled a gun!" Lucy said, spluttering.

"Henry acted to defend his sister," her father said. "But most won't see it that way. And I'm an outsider, so they may not listen to me." He smoothed out the frown notch between Lucy's eyes with his thumb. "For now, you can see them here." He clamped on his hat and left for the docks, avoiding her mother's irritated look.

Lucy mulled over how the incident might affect her, let alone the twins, as she rolled out biscuit dough and picked vegetables for their supper. She sought out her favorite chicken and put it on her lap, lulled by the sleepy clucking all around her. She was surprised to see both Quill and Henry approach. They were talking and laughing as though nothing had changed.

They followed the usual pattern. After the lesson, Lucy read from *Hunchback* about the deformed young man who longed to be a part of his town. How he watched from above, from the roof of the cathedral. Quill listened while she wove baskets to sell for her school materials. As the story progressed, Henry drew nearer and nearer until he was reading over Lucy's shoulder.

"Bad way to treat a guest," murmured Quill, when they got to a part where the young man summoned the courage to join the village festival, only to be teased and taunted by the crowd. Lucy read on. The young hunchback's hope turned to rage as the crowd tied him up and threw food at him, making him the object of their jeers and taunts—a fool for a day.

"He *is* a fool!" said Henry. "Why is he following *their* rules?"

"Shouldn't he?" asked Quill, glaring at her brother. "Even a fool has to follow some rules, in the end... to get along." Quill ripped out some of her weaving. "He needs to try again."

Lucy looked from one to another. She had a feeling they weren't talking about the Hunchback anymore.

Henry ground his heel into the dirt. "They won't let him."

Relief swept through Lucy when she saw her father appear from the woods.

"The news is bad in town," he said. "There have been a number of robberies, they think by the same man that broke into the pharmacy. You know that big one, with the scars on his arm? The Indian agent in town is concerned."

"Indian Agent?" Lucy asked. She'd seen the term in the newspaper.

He explained, "There's an agent in each community responsible for dealing with the local Indians, and he is particularly charged with preventing intoxication. Someone's started running illegal liquor to the tribe again."

Both Lucy and Quill looked at the ground, the sky, the trees, anywhere but at Henry.

"We'll just have to hope those men stay put at Port Discovery after the knife situation." He studied Henry, who kicked hard at the dust again. "They're looking for someone to blame."

"But Judge Swan knows the truth about those men," said Lucy. "You told him!"

"The judge will do his best to help," he said. "But things often go on outside the law," he turned to Henry. "Be Careful." He went inside, and Henry left shortly after.

"It's bad," said Quill.

"In town?" Lucy asked.

"In my brother," she said, and sighed. "I have seen him with that Indian. Uncle George is trading with him and my brother helps."

"Whiskey?" whispered Lucy.

Quill nodded, "My uncle is not a bad man, but he is not happy." She frowned. "He takes my brother with him."

"What will happen?"

Quill shook her head slowly, "You know that scarred Indian?"

Lucy nodded, feeling a chill.

"He killed one of us, a long time ago," Quill said. "We don't trust him. He doesn't care about your law, our law...anyone's law."

CHAPTER 15

Divided Loyalties

June ended and the Fourth of July approached. Lucy and her mother began rising with the sun to get their work done before it grew warm: sewing and preserving, starching and ironing and scrubbing. When they had a little extra time, they laid out squares for a baby quilt and pinned them together. It was the first her mother had made since she the little ones died. Their quilt was wrapped around the two of them in the coffin.

Lucy's quilt was Boston in spring, with the pink and white of cherry blossoms and a buttery yellow around the edge. It had been finished by the ladies on their street at a cheerful gathering. This new one had greens and blues like trees running downhill to the ocean. But who would help them stitch the layers together, and tack on that final strip of cloth for the binding?

One day, they were piecing the individual squares together into long strips that would be joined to form the top of the quilt. Lucy struggled to make the squares line up exactly so that the complicated pattern would work when the strips were connected.

Her mother said, "Are you listening to me?" Lucy looked up from her work.

"I said, Matthias' folks are having an Independence Day picnic next week." She spoke through a mouth full of pins as she smoothed a seam. "Matthias asked particularly if you were coming."

Lucy could feel her mother's eyes on her and flushed. "He hardly speaks to me!"

"You never know what's going on behind two eyes," her mother said.

"Oh, no, I can't!" Lucy said.

"Why?"

Henry had asked if she'd like to learn to dig clams, as it was something everyone did. She had to admit that she wanted very much to see him in action again—his quickness and fierce focus. When he'd asked, his half-smile had made her heart beat faster, and the way he looked into her eyes with an expression that was both shy and playful.

"I was to planning to dig clams, with Henry," Lucy said.

Her mother stretched and rubbed the middle of her back. "Matthias is a good son to his mother," she said, as though Lucy had not mentioned Henry.

"But what about Henry?"

Her mother sighed. "I don't know Henry's mother. The clams will still be there, Lucy... and you're not to go places with the twins, remember?"

The set of her jaw told Lucy it was hopeless. "Do we all have to go to the picnic?"

"Your papa's too busy with ships' work, and I need to rest."

Lucy plunked herself down on a chair. "Well, that settles it," she said, crossing her arms. "But no one would see us on the beach, if they're all at Matthias' farm." The minute she said it, she knew she'd gone too far.

"Young lady!" said her mother, shaking her finger at Lucy. "If you keep arguing with me, you won't be going to the Bishops' either!" Her mother spit out her pins, folded up the quilt, and slammed the kettle down onto the stove.

Now Lucy would be stuck at home on the Fourth of July! "How can we miss the only thing that's happened since we moved here... maybe since the town was founded?" she wailed.

"Wait a moment!" Her mother looked perplexed. "I thought you didn't want to go?"

"I never said that! Only that I wanted to go more, with—um—Quill."

"I was going to let you ride alone with Matthias. I trust that young man."

"Just the two of us?" A thrill ran up her back as she considered what Katherine might think about that prospect. "But, what will we say to each other?" asked Lucy in a panic. She'd never gone anywhere with a boy alone before. "Matthias and I? Isn't that a long ride?"

"He'll call for you after his milk deliveries. It's all arranged." A tired smile flitted across her mother's face. "It will be dark when you return, so someone will accompany you back. And Lucy?" A gleam of spirit returned to her mother's eyes. "Try not to enjoy yourself."

With a few days to get through before the party, Lucy kept herself busy doing chores and playing with Dodger. One day, she glimpsed a quick movement in the trees. Drawing a little closer, she could just make out Henry talking to someone in a ratty coat. The two parted, and as the other man passed by she got a glimpse of his profile. With a shiver, she recognized Katherine's father. She ducked when Altman jerked around and stared straight into the bushes where she was hiding. The hairs stood up on the back of her neck.

After a moment, he swore and stomped away. Had he seen her?

Tate Altman reminded her entirely of the men at Discovery Bay. The image of the mill workers merged with Altman holding his gun in her mind, as she crouched in the bushes. She stood up and shook her head, trying to clear the thought. It was replaced by an equally awful one that had haunted her dreams: Katherine, holding up the murdered book and gloating.

Lucy thought about rum running. Her father said it was a crime to sell liquor to the Indians, but people did it anyway, making a shameful profit off them. She couldn't understand the whole thing. It seemed everyone down on Water Street was getting plenty of rum, especially the sailors. The newspaper was filled with ads for liquor coming in by boat: Whiskeys, Porters and Pale Ales. By the pint or the quart, by the case or by the dozen, Port Townsend was well supplied.

"It can be like a poison," her father had explained. "Poison if we get too much, and much worse for the them. The Indians have no experience with it. They might drink too much, get wild, sometimes even throw away all their things. It's like they've lost themselves."

"How awful," Lucy had whispered.

Her father had nodded grimly in agreement. Then he'd looked sideways at her...an odd look, and she'd felt suddenly uneasy. Her father shocked her by saying that someone he loved had died young because of drink, but he wouldn't say who.

Lucy had seen men drunk in Boston, especially around the waterfront. Sometimes, they'd seemed happy and a little silly, pushing each other off the docks and into the water. But sometimes they staggered, and retched, and couldn't talk the way they should. She thought about her grandfather, who'd died young. No one spoke much about him.

Lucy stood in the trees long after Altman was gone. She'd have to ask more about her grandfather. And what about Henry? She didn't think he had ever been in the drink when she was with him. But he had definitely been carrying something for Altman.

Quill's words came back to her: "Sometimes, I wish Henry wouldn't help."

Two days before the party, Quill came for a lesson. When Lucy asked where Henry was, Quill pressed her lips together and said nothing. Lucy and her mother had done all the chores early so the girls were free, but not truly free. Lucy knew she wasn't allowed to leave the clearing with her friend.

After lunch, they lolled in the grass while Dodger nibbled. They wove clover into rings, and Lucy placed a crown of daisies on Quill's shining river of black hair.

"My mother was a princess," said Quill, understanding the word better now. "As a chief's daughter, she was...important. And beautiful!"

"Which would you rather be?" asked Lucy.

"Beautiful!" Quill laughed and sat up straighter. "Like my mother. You?" Quill wrote a Q in the air and raised her eyebrows and Lucy burst out laughing. It was one of their jokes together from that first day learning letters. "You is spelled with an L!" Quill would say, and Lucy's answer was always: "No, you is spelled with a Q." Then Quill would write "Y-O-U."

"Important!" said Lucy. "I want to be as smart as smart can be. I want to *do* something." But, she had to admit to herself that being beautiful wouldn't hurt. She wondered what Henry might consider beautiful—with a sister and mother who were so lovely, and so different from herself. Lucy's mother's skin had been described as luminous many a time, as though she were a small moon walking the earth. Lucy hoped she had inherited her mother's lovely skin, but would Henry think her pasty-faced? She wanted to feel like a glowing moon, but she had to admit she usually felt like a clammy oyster.

What made someone beautiful? Both Henry and Matthias made her feel that she might be nice-looking, but in such different ways! She thought Henry liked her eyes, and how fierce she was with him; and Matthias seemed to like that he and she were much the same. But she wondered if Matthias would like her when she was running pell-mell down a sandy beach with Quill. And would Henry still like her in the school house, quiet and serious over her books?

The night before the party, Lucy's father called her outside to the porch. The sunset blazed on the giant firs and white-bellied swallows swooped over the grass and had loud disagreements on the ridge-line of the roof. They sat together, listening to the frogs as they started their nightly croaking, and the night jars with their many sharp clacks followed by a few trilled notes of song. The long-winged birds cut in close to the house, then veered away, their gray wings blending into the dusk.

"Lucy," her father said. "I wanted to tell you that you shouldn't mention Henry to Matthias." Her father had an uncanny ability to see inside Lucy. She'd planned to ask Matthias all kinds of things, including relations between the tribe and the settlers. But she hadn't thought of Henry as a particular topic. "Why?"

Her frowned. "Henry got into some trouble there."

"At Matthias' place?" asked Lucy. "Are you sure?" The Bishop family seemed kind and hard-working, and too busy with the dairy to waste time arguing with anyone.

"Do you remember when Matthias had to leave early the other day to help his father?"

She nodded.

"That was because of Henry."

Lucy's heart fell. She'd assumed Henry was away helping the scarred man with rum running. Now he'd found another kind of trouble. He seemed to have a talent. "What happened? He hunts for elk there, often."

"On Bishop's farm? What does that have to do with anything?" While she didn't want to think Henry could cause problems, her father sounded serious. "What happened?"

"I asked Judge Swan. I've been keeping my ears open downtown for any news related to Henry. This is what I found out—." He paused. "Our farmers raise large, slow animals," said her father. Lucy put her fingers next to her head like horns, but he didn't laugh. "Fences protect the pastures from the elk's huge feet; but they also keep them from their usual paths. And the hunters as well. The judge says that part of Chimacum around Bishop farm has been a tribal hunting place for countless years."

"There must be other places to hunt elk?" asked Lucy.

"It may look like open forest to us, but they see boundary lines. The Clallams, Chemakum, and the Snohomish—if one tribe hunts in another's territory, they break treaties, maybe even start a war. In their minds, these lands are all portioned out."

She nodded, trying to grasp what he was telling her.

Her father explained how Quill's uncle stopped his people from going to war not very long before. "It was a time when settlers were killed in other parts of the territory, by tribes that rose up. Chief Chetzmoka stood between the warriors and the settlers for many days, finally convincing his fellow Clallams not to attack."

"Oh, that's good!"

"It cost him, Lucy."

"Cost who?"

"Chetzmoka. Some of the tribe wanted to claim their hunting and fishing lands back. Some lost faith in him for cooperating with the settlers. They hadn't seen what he had in San Francisco: the might of the U.S. military."

Her father was a master of distracting himself mid-story, and left to write some notes about the night jars. Later, Lucy realized that he'd never finished the story about Henry at the Bishops', or about Chetzemoka. People praised their local tribe for being a peaceable lot, but Lucy could still feel the fear in town. She had no idea how Henry, the elk, a bull, and a fence connected, but she wanted very much to know.

CHAPTER 16

Alone with a Boy

The day of the picnic finally arrived. Lucy rose early, adding a new lace collar her grandmother had sent to her dress. She didn't know what to expect at the Bishop farm. "Matthias's milk and cream are sold as far away as Seattle!" Ruby would say, blushing any time the boy in question looked anywhere near her side of the room. The Bishops were prosperous, but what did that look like in Port Townsend? A larger log cabin, or perhaps a proper house like Mrs. Blanc's?

Downstairs, Lucy caught her parents whispering. They startled and moved apart when she appeared, and Lucy felt her excitement dampen. Her mother looked so tired. But she bustled about, wrapping a blackberry cobbler in a checkered cloth for Lucy to take, and then helping Lucy tame her hair. She sounded quite cheerful as she talked with Lucy about the day ahead.

"Hello?" Matthias called from the front door. He wore a new white shirt, and his broad shoulders looked like they might burst through. He cast an appreciative eye over the shining counter and stove, which made Lucy glad she'd scrubbed them so well the day before. While Matthias and her father discussed the hay crop, she busied herself collecting her gloves and kissing her mother.

"Matthias, I'm bound for the docks and the customs house," said her father. "Everyone's aflame to get to gold before the cold sets in!"

"It's a fever, sir," agreed Matthias. "Gold fever!"

"You found another kind of gold out there in Chimacum!" said her father.

"Yessir! The grass is rich for the cows, and everyone needs milk and cream," Matthias said, nodding his agreement. His eyes were on Lucy the whole time he was talking.

Matthias lifted Lucy into the wagon. Then he welcomed her and she thank-you'd him and they fell silent. *Don't ask, don't ask, don't ask,* Lucy told herself. They'd barely gotten past the woods and onto the streets of uptown before her question burst from her lips.

"What happened with the bull and the fence?"

Matthias looked surprised, but answered calmly. "Bull spooked, cows got hurt, fence got knocked over." He looked over at her, then flicked the reins. "That's about the size of it."

Lucy laughed at his short speech. "That doesn't sound too terrible."

He frowned. "It wasn't good. That bull cost us a pretty penny. He's our new breeder, and not very old; we just had him shipped down from Whatcom." Then a slew of words poured out of him like nothing Lucy'd ever imagined, about livestock and breeding and bloodlines. He looked into her eyes and smiled. "You try catching a bull once he's gotten loose. M-A-D!" He rolled his eyes and stomped like a crazy bull. Lucy couldn't help laughing.

"But that had nothing to do with Henry, right?"

Matthias' mouth compressed into a line. He hunched over the reins and Lucy began to wonder if she'd stepped right into a cow pie. Her father would be furious if he knew she'd brought the subject up, although she doubted he'd be surprised.

He let out his breath with a sigh. "I know who you're talking about, and he's trouble, always. This is what happened, if you really care to know: the other day he shot an arrow at a cougar and wounded it, but didn't kill it outright. The cougar tore through the cows, killing a heifer and her calf, then spooked our bull right through the fence. Henry's lucky the bull wasn't killed. We had to get the vet out for stitches. Papa told him not to come around anymore if he couldn't respect our property lines."

Remembering what the judge told her father, Lucy said, "But, those are *his* places."

"I didn't know you knew him so well," Matthias said, pulling back on the reins with a grunt. The horses stopped and looked back at Matthias as though wondering why they were stopping in the middle of the road. "Or that you knew so much about our land."

"Well, not so much," said Lucy, flustered. "Mostly, I know Henry's sister." That didn't seem to answer very well either. "I didn't mean to pry," she said.

He nodded and flicked the reins.

Still, she'd like to understand better. "Can I ask? What about the hunting places?"

"You mean our farm?" he asked.

"Well, yes," Lucy said, her words stumbling out.

"The government gave my father the heart of those lands. He paid for the rest with his sweat: Ten years raking and cutting, grubbing out rocks to build fences. We've cleared each pasture with toil," he said, flexing his knuckles, which were scarred and rough. "I've been picking rocks and making them into walls since I was knee-high to a chipmunk." He stopped the wagon again and turned to her. "Would you have us give all that away?"

Blast it! Only ten minutes into the ride and Lucy had wrecked the mood, and with the only person who spoke to her at school. She sat up, holding her back straight like a lady, and looked about as they headed down the ridge from uptown and then uphill again out of town. If she'd hoped to impress the girls from school, her timing was all wrong. The streets were empty. "Where is everybody?" she asked, trying to lighten the mood.

"I had to finish my chores before leaving. Some people are already out at the farm. And the others... " he shrugged.

Lucy caught an odd tone in his voice. "Isn't everybody coming?"

Matthias looked sideways at her, feeding the reins through his work-chapped hands. He blew out his breath. "Let me tell you a little bit about my father," he said. "It'll while away the time as we go." He seemed to have forgiven her for the Henry comments, and Lucy was glad for a way to pass the time. "Please!" she said.

"Papa was a deck hand on an English navy ship, which docked

in Victoria a number of years back after a long voyage. Poor as dust and worked to death, and that's when there weren't whippings! All the sailors had wasted away—nearly to sacks of bones. He and some friends decided to jump ship and find a new life." He caught her eye. "You have to understand. If they'd been caught, they'd have been hung from the mast as deserters." Lucy shivered.

"By some miracle he and his friends made it twenty miles across from Victoria in a small canoe, landed at Dungeness, and walked all the way here. You still with me?"

Lucy said yes, but it was hard to think on such serious thoughts with the swallows swooping around their heads and the Queen Anne's lace buzzing with bees along the roadside. Independence Day, and a drive alone with a boy! Lucy felt a thrill. There wouldn't be fireworks here, but the day seemed to hold possibilities. She tried to focus on Mr. Bishop's life story.

"Papa hired out as a laborer around town. When he was poor, everyone was kind—gave him work and food. He's grateful for that!" Matthias chewed on a long piece of grass he'd snagged when they wandered into the ruff. "But now he's the one doing the inviting, the prosperous one. Some can't fathom a hired hand owning such a big property."

"Figures!" said Lucy, putting her hands on her hips. In their little dot of a town on the backside of the world, you couldn't be too low, and you couldn't be too dressy, and you couldn't, couldn't, couldn't...

Matthias grinned at her. Then he shrugged his large shoulders. "We have other friends. And most folks seem content to pay for our cream! Besides," he drawled, "Papa raised the prices for certain houses, the ones that were particularly churlish in their comments."

Lucy laughed at the thought of some customers being charged a tax on their rudeness.

As they drove along, Matthias named the farms they passed and the families they belonged to. There were cabins and a few larger houses, but Lucy was totally unprepared for what lay ahead.

"There it is!" said Matthias as they crested a ridge. Looking down, Lucy rested her eyes on the prettiest farm she'd ever seen, here or anywhere. White fences enclosed green fields, which fanned out around a large red barn with a belfry and white vents in the roof. There were many smaller buildings as well. Above it all rose green foothills and blue mountains, all the way to the horizon. She'd rarely seen a prettier valley.

Matthias pointed out the water tower and the farm's other features, leading to the yellow house with its broad porch. Lucy counted at least ten windows in the upper story, and the bottom floor spread wide and deep. Pulled up in front were some twenty wagons.

"Pa invited all the farmers around, all the way down to Brinnon."

"That many people?" She had a panicky feeling.

He looked at her in surprise. "They're friendly folk, mostly here to help with the harvest."

The wagon rolled through the fields near the house. Herds of cows chewed grass on either side, their bells clanking, and saplings lined the fences. When the trees grew up, there would be a grand archway of branches over the lane.

"Cherry blossoms are beautiful in the spring," said Matthias, "You should come see!"

Lucy's cheeks warmed at the hint of another visit. Not knowing how to answer, she jumped down before Matthias had completely stopped the wagon. As she landed, she felt a prickly feeling along her neck, and turned in time to glimpse Katherine's skirts disappearing around the corner of the house. Her outlook for the day dimmed.

Matthias led Lucy along to the door, calling "Mama!" He brushed past Katherine with an irritated look when she stepped into his path. Lucy was not so lucky, and tripped over an unseen foot, stumbling into the kitchen. She smoothed her dress as a woman turned to greet them.

CHAPTER 17

Party at Bishops' Farm

Lucy gaped at the woman as she realized the obvious: Matthias' mother was an Indian. She'd always thought his dark skin was from working outside dawn to dusk. Mrs. Bishop wore a starched muslin shirt with a gray apron over the top, and her boots were supple, high-buttoned leather. She reminded Lucy powerfully of Mrs. Blanc, with her quiet colors and elegance, but she also wore one of the abalone clips in her dark hair, like the aunties on the island. It flashed silver, pearl and dusky blue when she turned her head.

"So pleased to meet you," she said, holding out her hand. "I hope you got a word or two out of my son while you drove?" she asked, as he fled the room.

A word or two? He'd talked non-stop! "No, I mean yes," said Lucy. "He was very nice."

Matthias' mother gave her a sympathetic smile, as though the two of them shared a secret, and Lucy suddenly felt more relaxed. She returned Mrs. Bishop's smile, grateful for the woman's kindly attitude. She wondered what Mr. Bishop would be like, and if Matthias took more after his father or his mother. He had her kindness, and that comforting sense of quiet strength.

Mrs. Bishop led her to a group girls sitting by a window in the front room. Lucy's stomach clenched. Entirely too many from school! She didn't know why she'd thought the Bishop Farm would be any different from town. If she were a boy, she'd be safe in the barn by now, holding a spitting contest, but she wasn't. She'd likely be stuck here all afternoon, listening to Katherine's opinion on everything from dill pickles to hairballs.

A slender, blue-eyed version of Mrs. Bishop stood and greeted Lucy. "Come see my room?" she asked, taking Lucy's arm.

Lucy gladly escaped the crowded parlor. She hadn't met Bekah before, as the girl was often sick and had a tutor for lessons. She was young, but Lucy didn't much care. She could have a second nose on her face for all Lucy cared, so long as she was nice.

In Bekah's room they looked over her games, books, and china dolls, some of which were nicer than Lucy's best. In the second parlor, they uncovered a beautiful piano.

"Do you play?" asked Bekah, as Lucy ran her fingers over the smooth keys.

"I used to," said Lucy.

"I'm learning from an old neighbor," said Bekah, making a face, "but I'm not very good."

"Well, I haven't practiced in months!"

"Please, play something for me," asked Bekah.

Lucy agreed, starting with *Für Elise*. A few sour notes made her cringe, but Bekah didn't seem to mind. Their piano in Boston had been her grandmother's, and shipping it out here would cost half a year's pay, even if her father were getting paid. She hadn't realized how much she missed her piano. As she played, her fingers relaxed and she quit looking over her shoulder for Katherine. Lucy started to float along with the music.

When she looked up, she found a ring of girls around her and her fingers paused over the keys. She thought of Quill, and decided to look a little closer. Lucy didn't know most of them, but many had admiring looks on their faces, so she kept playing. A small girl started spinning on the carpet, and the others formed a ring and danced faster and faster until they tumbled, laughing, onto the floor.

"Where's Katherine?" Lucy asked. No one seemed to know, or much care.

"Probably hunting my poor brother," said Bekah. She and Lucy exchanged a knowing grin.

Before lunch, Matthias's mother handed Lucy platters of sliced breads and pointed to bowls filled with fluffy butter. Her mouth watered. Only a few people in Port Townsend had enough money for butter and cream like this. Lucy's family had free milk as part of her father's teaching allowance. But it tasted so watery, she was sure the cows that gave it were mighty thin, or that all the cream had been skimmed off the top. She wondered if she could get her father to ask for better milk, for her mother's sake.

Matthias' father said a blessing, standing at the head of the long trestle table under a spreading apple tree. Watching the well-built man, Lucy had a hard time imaging the half-starved sailor who'd arrived by canoe. After the prayer, people passed around platters of smoked ribs, new potatoes drenched in butter, shelled peas, and bib lettuce fresh from the garden. Lucy sat down in the spot Bekah had saved for her.

Katherine had reappeared and wedged herself in the middle of the overall-wearing end of the table. Lucy didn't envy her, as they only seemed interested in one thing: their food. When they did talk, it was about the hay crop or the terrible war back East between the Northern and Southern states.

"Katherine dear, what are you doing down there?" asked Mrs. Bishop. "Come here, by me." Lucy was amazed when Katherine obeyed. Picking up her plate, the girl trudged to an open spot among the women. Matthias looked up at Lucy and winked, then went back to his potatoes.

Lucy had filled the last open space in her stomach with blackberry cobbler and cream, and her mind with gobbets of gossip about Katherine's mother. The ladies whispered that Mrs. Altman had run off a number of years before. When Katherine joined them they fell abruptly silent, and Lucy felt a moment of pity for the girl.

She thought of her own mother and worried that she might be trying to lift heavy things, or dig the potatoes. Half of Lucy would be content to stay at the Bishop farm forever, while the other half wanted to go straight home. *What if something happened to her mother while her father was down at the docks?*

Excitement shot through the gathering after dinner. "Come on!" called Bekah, as the women drifted after the men toward an oval track of freshly plowed dirt in the middle of a field. A straggly line of about twenty boys stood at the starting line, which had been drawn in the dirt. Someone had strung red, white and blue flags above the finish line. Matthias towered a head taller than all the others, with two lanky boys on either side of him.

"Who are they?" asked Lucy, pointing to the boys, who reminded her of Henry.

"The Brinnon boys," said Bekah, stretching her arms wide. "Their father has a biiiiig farm... first claim down on the canal." She explained that Mrs. Brinnon was one of Chetzemoka's sisters. Lucy looked over at the woman, who was standing next to Bekah's mother. Now, she could see the similarity to Quill and her aunties.

"She's lovely, isn't she?" Bekah said, voicing Lucy's thought. The woman had bright eyes, and a white smile. She threw back her head and laughed at something Mrs. Bishop had said, and Bekah chuckled too. "They've been friends since before I was born!" she said.

The two women were very different in build. Mrs. Brinnon looked strong and full of energy, while Bekah's mother was more slight. Bekah was chewing on a long piece of grass and spat it out to say. "They look so different—but inside?" she poked at her chest, "...it's like you took one heart and split it in two."

"Is your mother a Clallam too?" asked Lucy.

"Oh no," said Bekah. "Mother's Snohomish, and so I'm part Snohomish too." She gazed out over the fields as though looking far away. "Only a few, now." She opened her mouth as if to say more, but with a *crack!* the gun went off. The runners sped away, with dust flying behind their heels. They made a breeze all their own as they rushed by into the first turn. The pack began to stretch out, and parents and children crowded the makeshift track, cheering.

"Matthias! Go!" bellowed Bekah, deafening Lucy.

The oldest of the Brinnon boys edged ahead, but then Matthias' bare heels flashed in the dirt, kicking him forward with a surge.

He won the race with many lengths to spare, his arms high and a pleased smile on his face. He let out a whoop.

How could I ever have thought Matthias was quiet? And for his size, he was surprisingly fleet on his feet. "Wow!" Lucy said, and waved and clapped with the rest of the crowd.

Wheelbarrow races and backwards crab races followed. Some of the more spry old men peeled off their shirts, down to white undershirts and suspenders. With their long beards blowing in the breeze, they tossed hot potatoes back and forth while they scurried down the field. Bekah and Lucy took part in the egg relay. Lucy kept dropping the egg off her spoon. She and Bekah were soon laughing so hard as they poked among the bushes trying to find their egg, that they gave up altogether. By then, the farm had the sleepy feel of a hot afternoon.

While the adults dozed, the younger crowd took over the farm for hide and seek. Katherine kept jumping out, trying to be caught by Matthias, or punching those she wanted to eliminate. Or were those the ones she favored? It was hard to tell.

Lucy and Bekah climbed into a leafy hideout, whispering while everyone else was found. Lucy told the story about Quill's mother getting stolen away.

"Oh, I know! So sad," said Bekah. "When my mother was a girl, she had nightmares about getting kidnapped by the Haida." Her voice fell to a whisper. "They're a powerful tribe from up north, with the fastest canoes. You can't get away."

"What about the ones that killed Colonel Ebey?"

"I've heard about that," she said,"from Matthias. He admired Mr. Ebey so much. Wants to go into politics, like him. My dad says he chose some of the best farmland in the world when he claimed that strip of Whidbey." She looked around, and her voice dropped. "My mother doesn't like me talking about this. She says it stirs up bad feelings to no good purpose."

While the topic was very serious, Lucy was enjoying watching Bekah tell the story. She was easy going like her brother, but also wildly dramatic like Ruby. Lucy liked her, and wished she lived closer to town.

"Anyway, there was a fight at Port Gamble Mill. Some big canoes from the north landed on the beach, and then the people wouldn't leave. The northern tribes had been raiding more than usual that summer and the workers were afraid. So they stayed inside the buildings, including many S'Klallam who work there. A ship was called in and after some talking back and forth... who knows how it all started, but a sailor was shot and died. Well, then the ship raked that beach with cannon fire. My mother passed by... after." Bekah paused. "Said it was the worst sight she ever saw. An ugly thing."

Both girls were quiet for a moment.

"Still, poor Colonel Ebey," said Bekah. "What a mistake!"

"Why do you say that?"

"He wasn't even part of the Port Gamble mess. When warriors came back the next year for revenge, someone gave his name." Bekah shivered. "They wanted a different man—who was gone at the time—and took Colonel Ebey's life instead, to pay for their chief's life." She stared at Lucy for a moment. "Mother says it's their way of getting justice, like in the Bible when they say, 'An eye for an eye and a tooth for a tooth.' I sure wouldn't want to be that eye."

Lucy agreed, and was ready to move. She jabbed Bekah in the ribs. "Come on," she said, dropping to the ground. "Do you folks believe in tea around here?"

Bekah rolled her eyes at Lucy. "With two parlors, what do you think?"

They came back to the porch and found afternoon refreshments set out. Lucy sipped her tea, listening as first one and then another cricket chirped, and watched the sun slant across the fields, making long shadows of fence posts. She hadn't felt so content since they'd left Boston.

A few tuning notes from a fiddle rose and fell on the evening air. Lucy hadn't thought about a dance. In the barn there were chairs set up, a table with a water jug, and some ginger beer for the children, who sat on hay in a corner watching the men and women twirl by in a waltz. After a few songs, the fiddler said, "Let's kick it up a little!" Stomping and clapping rattled the rafters, and Lucy was sure if the floor planks weren't so thick they'd have broken through to the cellar below.

The smaller children danced a long snake, in and out of the swirling partners. Katherine glowered from the doorway. Why the girl thought someone would ask her to dance was a mystery to Lucy. There were plenty of older girls available who'd arrived late in the afternoon for dinner and the dance, girls with their hair up and pretty dresses on. Lucy was glad she'd dressed nicely, though her clothes were grass-stained from hide-and-seek. If she got invited again, she'd know to wear plain clothes for the day and bring nicer ones to change into.

Matthias hadn't yet appeared, but the Brinnon boys asked Bekah and Lucy to dance. They grabbed onto the serpentine and were pulled along until Bekah broke off to get some water, red-faced. None of them seemed embarrassed to be dancing with the younger children, and Lucy hadn't laughed or danced this hard for as long as she could remember. Even without fireworks, this was shaping up to be one of her best Independence Days ever.

Bekah introduced Lucy to William, the older of the Brinnon boys. He was tall and had a pleasant face and a wide, slightly crooked grin.

"Do you know Henry?" Lucy asked, "...and Quill?"

The young man choked on his biscuit at the mention of Quill. But his little brother said, "We're sort of cousins!" Lucy thought she would never get all of Quill's uncles and aunties, half-uncles and sideways connections straight.

Matthias arrived and cuffed William on the head. William slugged him back, in the way of comfortable friends. "Time to get Lucy home," said Matthias, nodding his head toward the team and wagon that stood waiting in the light that spilled from the barn door. Outside, the night had deepened to a blue-black hue.

Lucy hated to leave when she was having so much fun. Many of the visitors were planning to sleep in the house or barn that night, and the dance was winding up to full speed.

Matthias tilted his head as if in thought, then looked down at her. "First, I'd take a dance. If you'd let me," he said, with a bow.

Bekah's mouth fell open, and William grinned, saying, "Well? Answer the man!"

Nodding, Lucy took the hand that was offered her and was swept into a waltz.

Thank goodness I danced at school, even if it was with a girl! she thought, lifting the hem of her dress and following Matthias' lead as they swooped around and around the barn. Lucy found herself smiling into Matthias' eyes, and warming all along her ribcage—where his hand touched her side. For once, Katherine was nowhere in sight.

When she needed words most, Lucy had nothing to say, and the whole thing might have been embarrassing if they were simply standing, but a whole row of watchers flashed by every few moments: Bekah, William, his brother, and the younger children, all lined up against the refreshment table, grinning and pointing. When the music changed, Matthias dropped her hand and thanked her, turning her over to William. Lucy curtseyed. Then they were caught up in a square dance all the way up and down the barn, with every age and stage of folk folded in. Lucy knew she would be stepping lively in her dreams that night.

When Matthias broke in to claim Lucy for the ride home, Bekah protested, but Lucy thought of her mother's tired face. "It's fine," she said, "I'll collect my things." Lucy wandered out behind the barn and lingered for a moment, looking up at the sky. A shooting star streaked through the velvety sky, and then another and another, like fireworks.

Bekah raised enough of a ruckus that her mother let her serve as the chaperone. Lucy found out that Katherine had been their intended passenger, but had disappeared some time during the dance. Lucy heaved a sigh of relief. But she found herself wondering how the girl would get home, and what might be waiting for her when she got there.

Bekah hopped up onto the wagon seat and threw an arm around Lucy. Mrs. Bishop emerged from the house and Bekah gripped Lucy tight. "She might not let me go," Bekah whispered, "...the falling damps, you know." Lucy did know. Her mother was always fretting about the same thing if they were out past dewfall. Mrs. Bishop was carrying a wool shawl, which she insisted Bekah take in case of breezes. She wished Lucy a good night and asked her to pass on greetings to her parents. Then she rubbed each of the horses' noses, speaking softly to them. Lucy was fairly sure she was telling them to return safely with her children, but she couldn't quite catch the words.

As they rolled out of the yard, Bekah told Lucy that her mother was one of the few Snohomish left, and spoke her language mostly when she talked with the animals, or when she was very very angry. After a few sentences, Bekah yawned and fell asleep on Lucy's shoulder.

They left the farm with its pools of light behind, and entered the darkened fields beyond. A few stray notes of music and the occasional shout of laughter stayed with them, but were soon too faint to hear above the creaking sounds of the wagon as it swayed along. An owl hooted and the sound echoed, then faded. A moment later, a ghostly shape glided across the road ahead of them.

"It's hunting," Matthias said, as they watched it disappear into the darkness.

They bumped along in silence, lit by the kerosene lanterns hung on each side of the wagon. The lamps cast a dim glow around them.

"Penny for your thoughts?"

"I was thinking about the day," Lucy said.

"Good one, eh?"

"One of the best," she answered.

"Even better than Boston?"

Lucy paused. Was she hurting people's feelings by her constant talk of Boston? She suddenly felt ashamed of comparing everything and said, "Yes, even better!" She was glad he couldn't see her blush as she remembered the feel of his hand on her side while they danced. "Thank you," she whispered, knowing she was here because Matthias had wanted her to be.

The cool air and bright stars brought Lucy wide awake. She'd rarely been out this late at night, much less without her parents. She wouldn't waste a minute of it by falling asleep. The stars above them, blazing bright in the dark sky, the crickets, frogs and owls, and the occasional sleepy moo from the farms they passed...she hadn't expected to like it all so well.

"Want a story?" asked Matthias. "Bekah always asks for one right about here."

There was something nice, thought Lucy, about a big fellow like Matthias not thinking he was too old to tell stories. "I'd like that," she said.

He began: "Once there was a rich, young prince. He decided throw to a lavish party, and sent his servants out to all the castles and manors in the land. The cream of the cream!"

He grinned, and paused for effect.

It took her a moment. "Oh! Cream... you have a dairy." She laughed and playfully slapped his shoulder. "That's a terrible joke!"

"I have a million more like them," he said.

She had to admire how completely Matthias was a part of his home. He was a dairy farmer through and through. In a funny way, he and Henry both belonged to their places. She sighed. Had she ever even belonged to Boston in such a deep-rooted way?

Matthias looked at her.

"Anyway..." she prompted.

"No one would take him up on his offer. They all said no!"

"But why?" asked Lucy. "The prince must have had fabulous food, and music, and a magnificent ballroom..." She imagined being one of the people that got invited to Governor's Balls, and had dresses made for the occasion.

Matthias shrugged. "Who knows why they wouldn't come? They were too busy, or the feast wasn't important enough to them. They probably were bored with fancy food and good music and ball rooms." The horses had slowed and Matthias clicked his tongue and flicked the reins to get them moving again. "The Prince was angry at their lack of respect, and gave up on the cream of the cream. Then he invited the business owners and skilled workers of the town." He turned toward her.

"Did they say yes?" she asked, playing along.

"No. So, the Prince invited all who were left. He sent his men to the sick and lame and blind, those who lived in the streets or slept out in the fields under the sky. And?"

"And they all came, and had a fabulous time."

He laughed. "Yes, miss, they did. Of course when the others saw how wonderful the party was, they wished they'd said yes."

Lucy knew the tale well enough. The Prince was Jesus. She wasn't much of a Bible reader, but she thought it fitting to the day and to Mr. Bishop's story: He'd invited everyone from the sheriff to the people who picked his hops. Some refused his invitation, but Mr. Bishop didn't seem to worry about that. Everyone who came seemed happy to be there, and the food... oh, the food! Her mouth would water at the memory for weeks. Could she have been happier in a big ballroom than in the enormous barn, smelling sweetly of cedar and fresh hay, with the riot of dancing feet? She thought not.

They were quiet for awhile. Then they chatted about Port Townsend and Chimacum and the farm, while the miles rolled by under the wagon wheels. "Matthias?" Lucy asked, "Maybe I should pretend to know less than I do, to make people feel more comfortable with me." So many times, Katherine had told her, "You think you're too good for us."

"Whoa! Where'd that come from?" he asked. "My father would still be a hired hand if he thought that way, or a skinny sack of bones at sea." She felt a hand on her shoulder. "Be yourself. They'll get used to you in time."

She didn't like the idea of someone having to "get used to her," like an ill-fitting pair of boots. She wanted to slide right into a group of friends like she had with Emily and her sisters the first time they'd met on the sidewalk. She'd been invited to jump rope and that was that.

They were nearing town and Lucy felt a stab of regret that the day was drawing to a close. They traveled around the lagoon at the far end of the beach, past the high nets used to catch birds. The moon had risen, its reflection broken up in the reedy water near the S'Klallam houses. She wondered if Quill and Henry would ever fit in town. She was reminded of the hunchback in her book, wanting so much to take part in the life of the city around him.

The wagon pulled past the quiet houses where Quill's people were sleeping. The sentence slipped out before she could catch it: "Matthias, if your father is so welcoming, why did he tell Quill's brother to stay away from your farm?"

And so the lovely day ended as it had begun, with an awkward question and a tense reply. Matthias explained why Henry was considered a criminal around their farm, then fell silent. But it was not the friendly silence they'd shared before. She tried very hard to make up with a warm thank you as they reached her house, but Matthias did not respond.

The wagon creaked to a halt. Lucy gently shifted Bekah onto the seat. She moaned in complaint, and then curled up fast asleep. Matthias covered his sister with a blanket and jumped down, then lifted Lucy by the waist. For a moment, she felt like she was floating as he sailed her up and over the cart wheel, and lighted her down on the grass. Breathless, she clutched his sturdy arms for balance before stepping away. They stood for a moment, a few feet apart.

A familiar scent wafted toward Lucy from the front porch. Her father was waiting in the rocker, but he rose in no particular hurry to greet them. He trailed tobacco smoke and whispered that Lucy's mother was asleep. Matthias tipped his hat, greeted him, and smiled. When he included Lucy in his grin, she had a feeling he'd forgiven her the awkward questions.

Matthias climbed up and drove away whistling, with the moon splashing over his cart and casting shadows onto the roadway.

Lucy's dreams that night were a sweet swirl of dancing motion. As she fell asleep, the thought came to her that this had been the high point of her whole year. Then the unwelcome thought barged in: Everyone knew which direction things went after the peak.

CHAPTER 18

Burial at Sea

A new lease on life" is what her mother would call Lucy's mood the next morning. She threw open the window to welcome the light rippling across her shutters. The birds sang, the world was all abuzz and on the wing, and Lucy wanted to be outside too.

As she pulled on her old dress, she considered the night before. She hadn't realized she'd had a clock spring coiled inside her chest until she'd arrived back home from the Bishop farm. She'd felt it uncoil when she heard that her mother was peacefully asleep, and woke with the sense of a worry eased.

Nothing ill-fated belonged after a day like yesterday. Lucy bundled the scarred book into an old apron and tied it with a rope. She crept down the stairs, grabbed a biscuit and hurried outside. The meadow was tipped with dewdrops and the water spread like glass to the horizon. All was as it should be.

Winding down the path, Lucy kept an eye out for people in the trees. She saw no one as she wound down to the semicircle of sand directly below their house. The beach basked in the morning sun, and Lucy felt a strength in the light that had been missing until now.

As she approached the point, the water rippled. Across the way, she could see the green of Ebey's farm. On a day like today, it was hard to believe anything sorrowful had ever happened there. In between, Lucy knew, the water concealed a clash of currents that had caused grief to many a boat.

Pulling the bundle out of her bag, she selected four large stones, weighted it, and bound it about with twine. She didn't look at the book inside, having no desire to see Katherine's work ever again. She pulled off her shoes and stepped into the water.

"Carbuncles!" she yelled, making a seagull lift and squawk in alarm. "That's cold!"

No wonder she never saw anyone sea bathing! Lucy waded out until she was up to her knees. "It's cold as the Delaware at Christmas out here!" The seagull lifted backwards a few feet and let out a chattering sound like a laugh. "Wonderful!" muttered Lucy. "Another local, mocking me!" They'd surely think she was crazy if anyone knew what she was up to this morning. *Well, they needn't know.*

Pulling her arm back in a wide arc, Lucy swung the horrible memento faster and faster, and then cast the lump a good thirty feet beyond her. It splashed, floated for a moment on the surface, and then sank with a loud gurgle. She said a prayer, and was caught by a stitch in her ribs—a sudden sense of loss. In spite of what the girls in town thought, she had very few things of her own. The book had been so beautiful and crisp, such a nice gift from Mrs. Blanc.

Lucy was reminded of a strange night on their trip from Boston, off the coast of South America. It had been too hot to sleep, and she'd been on deck searching for cool air. As she admired the stars burning against the silky black sky, she'd suddenly become aware of a group of sailors at the back of the boat. She'd crept closer and heard the sailmaker give last rites over the cook's boy, who'd died of an infected wound. After a few words, they slid his body over the side. She'd just seen the boy the day before, dumping spoiled vegetables off the stern. He'd shown her a cut he'd gotten cleaning fish that had swollen and oozed. Then he was gone, sinking into the waters in his shroud made of sail cloth. The night had been quiet once more, and the cold stars had blazed on above them. The water had made a hushed sound against the side of the boat as they'd gotten under way again, leaving him behind.

It was right, the sailors said, to give lost things to the deep. Then you had to sail on.

The swallows chirped around her, skimming close over the

water and flicking their wings against the surface. Lucy filled her lungs with salty air and let the morning lift her. Then she ran back to the shore, whacking the surface of the water with her hands as she went, and churning with her feet. She kicked at the surf's edge and did a handstand, dripping glops of wet sand, and then launched into a water-logged cartwheel.

The book was gone! Katherine still lived, but her handiwork had sunk, and so had her control over Lucy. A gleam of malice riffled the surface of her peace. She couldn't help feeling a hint of triumph that Matthias had danced with her yesterday, and not Katherine.

As she climbed from the beach, she took one last look and her eye caught something in the driftwood at the high-water line—an object. As she drew near, she realized it was a boot, neck down in the sand. Ruby had told her that nothing disappeared forever in the Straits, but would cast up months, or even years, later. "The sea gives up her dead," she'd said, her voice aquiver with doom. "That's why they put lead weights in the bottom of burial sacks."

It was Lucy's boot! Cast up again after all these weeks, cracked and battered. She didn't dare touch it, knowing it for what it was— an omen. But what kind?

The boot was driven from her mind as Lucy reached home. Matthias stood before the front door, hand raised to knock. Lucy felt the flutter that came with a boy visiting, and not twelve hours after leaving her the night before! Then her steps slowed to a halt. Matthias was not alone.

In the middle of the top step, square in the way of anyone walking there, sat Henry. Just Henry, with a glower and a jaw that would have done Atlas proud. He held nothing in his hands but Quill's *McGuffey Reader*... no bow or bag or small animal. While Lucy watched, he turned his face toward Matthias' back, the gaze so intense she half expected Matthias' vest to sprout two burn holes. But Matthias acted as if he had the porch all to himself. The boys were so busy not noticing each other that they didn't see her.

Other than glimpsing him in the trees with Tate Altman, Lucy hadn't seen Henry in weeks. Her heart surprised her by doing a dance at the sight of his lanky frame on her porch, even as she was painfully aware of the disagreement she'd had with Matthias about him. Lucy wondered what she was supposed to do about the situation.

Henry caught sight of her first and bounded down the porch. He stopped short of her and planted himself, like he had the day she'd offered him cookies.

"Is Quill all right?" Lucy asked. He'd never come without her before.

"Yes." He ran his fingers through his hair, scratching himself with the book he forgot he was holding. "She made me come today."

"Why?" Something didn't fit. Why wouldn't Quill come as well? She never missed a lesson. Lucy ached to know what was going on in Henry's mind, wishing he would unwind his own coiled spring and really talk to her. She felt Matthias' eyes on her.

"Is she coming later?"

Henry gave his usual shrug, then tipped his head toward Matthias. "What's he doing here?" An inkling was starting to quiver at the edge of Lucy's mind. She turned back enough so she could see Matthias, whose head was slowly swiveling between herself and her father, who'd answered the door in his night shirt. Both men, young and middle-aged, turned and watched her with their arms crossed over their chests.

"I think you'd better go, Henry," she whispered. "But can you come back later, please?"

Henry glared back over his shoulder at the house, and tossed the reader onto the grass at her feet as he passed. The expression in his eyes reminded her of Dodger when he was driven into a corner by the hens. "Henry, wait!" she called, stooping to pick up the book. But he'd already disappeared.

She went to greet Matthias, who'd brought a special cream delivery. The night before, Mrs. Bishop had said, "Your mother could use some fattening." Before Lucy could get to him, Matthias handed her father the jar, stomped down the steps, leapt onto the buckboard of his wagon, and left.

Her father stood on the porch, holding the jar and staring at her with an odd expression. "Lucy, what in the blue blazes was all that?" She shook her head, wondering if she should try and explain the ins and outs of Matthias and Henry, or if she even understood it all herself. Luckily, he was distracted by the state of her clothing.

"You'd better change that wet dress before your mother wakes up!" He looked down and groaned. "And for mercy's sake, don't let her see those boots. Weren't they white at one time?"

That evening, with Dodger on her lap, Lucy added to her journal entry from the night before. Under a sketch of Matthias and the Brinnon boys running like hayfire through the fields she wrote:

Matthias gets along fine with my parents, and runs like the wind. Can't say I mind having the boy everyone likes as my good friend. I've never seriously liked a boy before. Maybe I'm too young to know about such things, but I don't feel that shiver up my spine that I've read about in books, or the hairs standing up on the back of my hands like Ruby's sister said I would.

Henry came by today, he said because Quill sent him, but I don't believe that. When I spied him on the porch, I could swear he was studying that reader purely for himself. He had his tongue out the side of his mouth, the way he does when he's setting a fish hook, or stringing a bow. I like the way he looks when he's thinking: all quiet, but blazing at the same time. I truly hope he doesn't feel replaced by Matthias at our house.

Matthias and Henry. If I had to choose between the two, which would I keep and which would I lose?

CHAPTER 19

Weaving and Fraying

Quill arrived early the next morning. She pointed at herself. "I'll be the teacher today," she said. "We will make a basket!" She sounded so happy at the thought.

"Oh no!" Lucy said, dismayed. She'd tried to make baskets on her own and the sad corpses lay in the bottom of the chicken coop—lumps of twigs and grass that the chickens had scratched to bits. She'd been much too ashamed to show them to Quill.

Quill insisted. "We're leaving in a few days to go down to the summer fishing grounds: the place you call Hood's Canal." She explained that they'd be catching and smoking salmon, their main food for the long winter ahead. They would be gone many days.

Lucy disliked the flatness in Quill's eyes. "But you'll be back!" Lucy said, poking Quill to try and prompt a smile.

Quill said, "We should take the opportunity to weave now, today."

"Goodness!" Lucy said. "You would not have said *opportunity* a few months ago!"

"Watch me," Quill said, pointing at the materials she'd brought. She submerged long strips of cedar bark in warm water. "It's not the right time of year. These are very dry," she said, "but I want you to know how." After they softened the strips, the girls used them for a framework and then added grasses, pushing them down in tight rows. Quill's fingers constantly interrupted Lucy's as she showed her how to twist here, break there. How to pull the bark in tight and how to start again, and again, and again.

"Remember," Quill said with the first smile of the day, "Q is for Quail! If I can learn that, you can learn this!" She studied Lucy. "Or don't you want to?"

"No, I do. Truly!" Lucy groaned and flexed her fingers.

Quill looked down at Lucy's basket. With its bark bulging, Lucy thought it looked more like a crow's nest than the smooth cup on Quill's lap. Her hands helped Lucy's once more, showing them how to move with the strands, not against them.

As she did, Quill wove her a tale of the cedar. "The trees stand deep in the forest, soaking up water and wind." She spoke with a rhythm that was soothing. "Each woman has a tree and visits it in the winter, when the bark is moist and soft. She pulls long strips from the tree, all the way up from the bottom as high as she can reach." Quill stretched her arms over her head and showed Lucy the heavy yank it took to separate the bark from the tree. "But she never takes too much. She pays attention to the life of the tree giving the bark," she said. "Only what is needed."

Her voice became sorrowful. "Your loggers have cut down so many trees. Some were my aunties' trees." Her voice became very quiet. "One was my mother's. It was to be mine."

Over those few peaceful days that hung between what had been and what would soon come, Lucy's baskets coiled into smoothly woven cups (though she knew they'd never be as fancy as Quill's with their flowers and birds). Her weaving progressed much slower than Quill's reading had, as she struggled to make her fumbling fingers do what Quill had shown her. In their school, Quill would be the brightest pupil—that is, if she could come.

Lucy thought of the hunchback, watching life from the roof of the giant cathedral after he'd been humiliated down below. Up there, the crowd couldn't reach you or hurt you. But this Lucy knew from experience: it was safe, but very lonely.

Henry did not visit again after the morning on the steps, and Lucy felt an odd echo about the place without him. She wondered if he was avoiding Matthias, who stopped by every morning to drop off milk with thick yellow cream on top. Her mother complained that they had more cream than they could use in a month of Sunday teas, but with a smile in her eyes. When Quill was there, she watched Matthias' trips up and down the steps with raised eyebrows. Lucy ignored her. She didn't want to talk about it, especially with Henry's sister.

When Quill left for the salmon run, Lucy sorely missed her help with the chores. The bigger her mother's middle grew, the shorter her temper became. She wanted everything washed doubly, even things that didn't look dirty. While Lucy scrubbed, her mother stitched little white garments, spending hours on a christening dress and its cap. Lucy felt a stitch in her heart, remembering the two white dresses she'd helped make for the early-born twins.

No, she thought firmly, *not this time*. In a few days there would be a quilting bee, and all the ladies would gather to help her mother sew the layers together, patterning the top with their stitches. She tried to imagine her brother or sister under it, hoping good thoughts would bring a healthy birth. But it was hard to see a different outcome to the one they'd always had. If anything, they were in a worse place.

In between lay Lucy's fourteenth birthday. She thought of Emily's fabulous party with a pang. It had qualified as an *Event of Note* in the society column in the newspaper, happening right before Lucy left. Emily's cousins had come all the way from New York. They'd eaten fairy cakes in a garden lit by paper lanterns, like the painting *Moonlight on Lilies*. Lucy had worn her new white boots and they'd been perfect. Boots. Lucy pictured her poor boot on the shore, worn and split, and Katherine with her big toes protruding from her famous clunkers. She sighed.

Her life was so dull here. She could only write about cooking and scrubbing and the vegetable garden. Her mother was swollen and short-tempered, her father working endless hours, and everyone interesting was away. As far as she knew, her birthday would be nothing to write about either. If she were lucky, she'd get *Tea with Chickens and Rabbit;* and no one was going to print that in a society column. Did *The Register* even have one?

Scrubbing the kitchen floor was even worse than what Lucy had imagined for her big day. After a quick kiss, her father left for the docks. Her mother sat frantically piecing the quilt so it would be ready for the bee. Lucy sighed.

No "Happy Birthday!" was wished. Nothing was said about a special meal, or a cake. Lucy decided she'd rather not think about what day it was. Maybe if she pretended this was any old day, it wouldn't be such a let-down. At least it wasn't like that other day—the twin babies' birthday—when the house was heavy with silence. She'd only seen it once, but Lucy knew her mother kept a death-day picture of them in her drawer.

In her mind, she went down the short list of friends she had here. Quill was gone. Henry was gone. Matthias was too complicated! Bekah was out in Chimacum and no way to get here, even if she wanted to. Ruby was sometimes friendly, but only when not around Katherine. Everything ended with Katherine.

"Lucy, you're scrubbing all the finish off those boards!" her mother said.

Lucy looked down. She'd worn a bare spot and would have to replace the beeswax. She racked her brains. Mrs. Blanc had gone to Olympia after her brother's scalp had been returned. She'd gotten tired of everyone's stares and whispers and gone to visit a friend, but now she was back. "Can I go see Mrs. Blanc?" she asked her mother, who was picking at a wayward stitch.

"I suppose," her mother replied, without looking up. "But go see your father first. He needs help with some errands." She looked up long enough to say, "Lucy, you're an eyesore! Put on your nice dress and brush your hair."

Lucy grumbled her way up to her room, then muttered her way into her nice dress. She'd look silly prancing around midday. Every other soul would be in work clothes. But once she was outside, her hopes began to rise. Her father might bring her a gift from town later. But no, she told herself, that was too much to expect. The port was a-clang with activity, he was busy, and they needed the money to pay for the doctor when the baby came.

With Mrs. Blanc's house on the bluff so near the stairs, Lucy couldn't help gazing in the windows as she walked by to see if anyone was home. She spotted Matthias' cart. *Strange, he didn't usually deliver at this time of day.* She walked slowly down the long flight of stairs to the waterfront, coming to a halt in the middle. She almost turned around. It would be so nice to have a conversation with someone close to her own age, but she didn't want to appear forward.

"What are you doing here?" her father asked, when she reached his office. He glanced at her, then went back to studying his papers.

Happy Birthday indeed! Lucy almost said, but managed to bite her tongue. Tears edged into the corners of her eyes. "Mother sent me to see if you needed help, before I visit Mrs. Blanc." Even to her own ears, her voice sounded quavery.

The judge wasn't there to give her a mint, or wish her joy on her day, or find an item in his collection for her—an old cigar box for Emily's letters, or a stone arrowhead.

"Errands, eh?" her father asked slowly.

He rummaged around his messy desk. Then his eyes lit up, and he handed her a packet of papers. "The new customs forms!" he said. "You can save me a heap of time by giving all the captains a copy, with my compliments." He handed her a nickel, as he always did. Lucy waited, giving him a chance to say something. Before she'd even left the room, he was back at his books.

She heaved a sigh and slammed the door shut behind her with a bang that raised the head of every newspaper-reading gentleman in the foyer.

In spite of it being her birthday-but-not-a-birthday, Lucy found herself enjoying the waterfront. As she went along, she smelled the warm pitch-on-logs scent of newly built docks, and listened to the slap of waves along the ships' sides. The sun warmed her hair and there was a salty tang to the air. Better than scrubbing, she had to admit. More than one young sailor tipped his hat as she strolled alongside the boats and delivered the forms. It made her glad she'd taken the time to change out of her grimy work clothes and brush her hair.

She reached the last ship and walked up the gangway. "I'll pass the papers on, Miss." A saucy young man, not much older than herself, stood barefoot on the deck. He squinted at her in the bright sun and pushed his cap back to scratch his head. "Didn't they already bring those papers... yesterday?"

"I don't know, I'm sure!" said Lucy, confused, and fled to the Mercantile, where she bought herself hard lemon candy to share with Mrs. Blanc. It was tradition to put the drops in their tea after a difficult lesson. Lucy thought today qualified as a difficult lesson.

There was no one from the tribe around town today. Now that she knew so many of Quill's relatives, it felt empty without them. But to Lucy's mind, the place felt more relaxed, too. She caught a paper blowing along the dirt of Water Street and smoothed it out.

Chimacum: Break In!

Grain alcohol was stolen from a store shed, and a horrible fire started that caught the house nearby and burned it to its foundations...

The writer blamed the fire on the local tribe, though reading carefully Lucy could see no proof. Right below, as though to link the two together:

Editorial: Begging the Indian Question

"Haven't we waited long enough? The tribes signed the Point-No-Point Treaty almost ten years ago. The land is needed for building, now. It's time for them to move out!"

The writer also hinted that certain "ne'er-do-well" persons might be responsible for pretty much every problem from sick cows to bad weather. The tone came near to hate, and made Lucy feel uneasy. It reminded her of the way people in the northern states started speaking of those in the South, right before war broke out between them.

When the newspaper blew out of her hands with a freshening breeze, she didn't chase it down. She wanted to enjoy a few moments of happiness on her birthday. Lucy dawdled among the boats. She'd been practicing putting her hair up, and she was knotting it around her fingers when she heard voices nearby. She snuck along the side of the ship until she was around the back end from them.

"*You'll* certainly miss their business, now, won't you?" someone said.

The answer was a grunt.

"They've overstayed their welcome," another said. "This will help them understand that."

What was *this?* Lucy wondered. She had a pretty good idea who *they* were.

"You hear something?"

Too late, Lucy realized she'd spoken the thought, and clapped her hand over her mouth.

"Nothing but your stomach!" the speaker said, with a knocking that sounded like a pipe being hit on a heel.

"Well," one said, then paused. She heard the intake of breath that went with a pipe being relit. "The place is an eyesore. We all know the kinda things that go on at that end of the waterfront." Sounds of agreement followed.

Which end of the waterfront? Lucy guessed they spoke of Quill's village, but plenty of things went on at the saloon end of town as well. She ran back along the ship until she was far enough away for a casual walker. She stepped out and curtseyed to the men in the smoking-knot, shivering when she met a familiar glare from their midst: Katherine's father, Tate Altman.

"Hey, you!" Altman yelled. Lucy bunched up her skirts and fled.

She took the stairs two at a time, but the bluff didn't seem to be getting any closer as she ran up the long flight. Then footsteps, loud on the stairs behind her. Her heart pounded in her ears as she turned to see who was following her. Her father? What was he doing out of the office at this time of day? She waited to see if something was wrong.

"Going... to Mrs. Blanc's," he explained, breathing hard. "I've, well." He held up a hand. "One moment!" When he'd caught his breath he said, "I've some papers for her." He motioned for Lucy to go ahead of him.

Lucy sighed. She'd wanted to ask Mrs. Blanc about the things she'd just heard. As well, she wanted to tell her all about birthdays in Boston and how disappointing this one was turning out to be. Her father would only get in the way.

"I'll wait for you here, then, if you have business to discuss," said Lucy.

"Oh, no need for that. Come along!" he said, and hurried past her. She glared at his back, but trudged up the steps after him.

The house seemed deserted. Matthias' wagon had left and Lucy wondered why Mrs. Blanc didn't come out to meet her, as she usually did. *Perhaps she's overcome with despair over the scalp*, she thought, stepping quietly on the porch floorboards. She wondered if she'd find Mrs. Blanc in a sad state, with her hair messy or her skirt wrinkled. *Maybe even drinking liquor!*

Her father opened the screen door and Lucy followed him. "Mrs. Blanc?" Lucy called. "Mrs. Blanc?" she said again, her heart beating faster in her chest. "Are you all right?" She couldn't see well in the dim interior. A floor board creaked, and then...

"SURPRISE! Surprise, Surprise!"

People flew out of every door and closet in the house. Mrs. Blanc, Judge Swan, Matthias and Bekah appeared, even her mother—who was red in the face like she'd just hurried up the path. "I fooled you!" her mother said. She turned to Mrs. Blanc. "You should have seen her face, scrubbing that floor!" She was laughing so hard, tears were running down her cheeks.

Lucy stood gaping at the smiling faces until her father took her shoulders and pointed her toward the table. A four-layer white cake held the place of honor, with scallops of cream frosting, topped with the words "Happy 14th Birthday!" She tried to take it all in: wrapped presents, china plates, silver forks, the best tea service, and everyone in their Sunday best. Once again, she was glad her mother had made her change.

"Happy Birthday, dear!" Mrs. Blanc handed her a parcel tied with a silver satin bow. "Straight off the steamer from San Francisco!" she said, beaming. Sitting down, Lucy unwrapped the package slowly, savoring the feel of the thick paper. Out rolled a ladies' parasol and a pair of fine gloves to match, with pearl buttons and loops for closure.

Lucy was speechless. Mrs. Bishop and her mother smiled.

"She'll look so stylish!" said Bekah, and handed Lucy a narrow packet in brown paper. "From Matthias and me," she said. Both of them were watching her closely. Inside nestled a branch with a root ball. "It's a cherry tree!" said Matthias, "The kind with the pink blossoms." Lucy thanked them sincerely, inviting them to come help her plant it, soon. The tree would be a lovely reminder of her day at the farm. She blushed as she felt Matthias' gaze on her.

Judge Swan handed her a square basket with a lid. Without being told, she knew that Quill had woven it. Inside hid another basket, and another, with the last shaped like a clam. It was a miracle of design. In the middle, she found a handful of limpets. Lucy fingered the shells, and felt a thrill in her middle. They brought back sun and salt and water, and Henry whispering in her ear. She blushed again, hotter.

The judge cleared his throat and pulled out a package. He smiled at her. Inside white butcher paper, she found her drawing of the hummingbird nest—nicely framed. "For the naturalist," read the card. She smiled back, amazed at how fine it looked under glass.

Now, her mother's turn: "I wasn't sick that day of the Bishop party." She and Lucy's father exchanged a look. "I had to finish this!" She handed Lucy a soft bundle. When she parted the layers of tissue, Lucy felt totally ashamed of herself for thinking she'd been forgotten. Inside, she found a corduroy dress crafted with tiny stitches, in periwinkle blue.

"Perfect!" said Mrs. Blanc. She held the dress up to Lucy. It dropped in flat tucks to her hips, and was indeed perfect. Nice, but not too fancy. Lucy twirled, letting the dress flare with her. She stopped to give her mother a loud kiss on her round cheek. This explained why she'd fallen so far behind with piecing the baby quilt.

Last, her father's gift: a blank book like the one Judge Swan used, but larger. The cover was rich red leather with a flap to protect the golden-edged pages. She ran her hand along the back, where her name was engraved, and the year: 1862. "For sketching," said her father, handing her a smaller box with an ebony pencil set inside. He watched her, puffing furiously at his pipe. Some of his hours of work at the docks must have been for this, Lucy realized. She reached around his neck, pen, journal, and all, and squeezed him hard.

They ate cake and drank tea from Mrs. Blanc's bone china cups, and no one seemed in a hurry to leave. Even the weather cooperated, giving them a rare calm evening with no wind and smooth water as far as the eye could see.

As she gave Mrs. Blanc a kiss goodbye, the lady said, "A better year ahead, yes?" Lucy nodded. Mrs. Blanc turned to her mother. "God Bless you, dear," she said, "I'll see you in a few days, at the quilting bee!"

Matthias was seeing to his horse. "Thank you, for everything," said Lucy shyly. She put her hand out to stroke the horse's neck and felt his big hand on her own. Before he left to get his sister, he leaned toward her for an instant. He was half way to the house before Lucy realized he'd kissed her cheek—the slightest brush of pressure, like a moth drifting past in the night.

On the path home, Lucy fell behind in the trees. She listened to the quiet of the wood and her parents' voices mingling together in the dusky air, with one hand held up to her face.

CHAPTER 20

Everyone's Invited, Unfortunately

The day of the quilting bee they rose before the sun to bake scones and roll sandwiches. Matthias knocked on the front door at dawn, with a jar of cream in his hands. The white liquid glowed in the early light. Lucy opened the door and they stood staring at each other.

"Bekah's laid out with a cold," he said abruptly.

"Oh, no!" Lucy had been counting on Bekah for moral support. All the mothers from town were coming, and she was sure Katherine would turn up too, like a bad penny.

"So many girls," she murmured.

"As there should be, at a quilting!" he quipped. "Myself, I'll be mucking out the barn!" He left to finish his deliveries, after pressing her fingers with his hand. She appreciated the gesture, but was distracted by thoughts of Katherine.

"Lucy, start the tea," her mother called. Lucy pulled out a fresh brick of Ceylon and crumbled some into the teapot, while her mother unwrapped the few china cups that hadn't been broken on the boat. "Wake up, Lucy!" her mother said. "Perhaps water, too?"

An hour later, Lucy's arm was near ready to fall off after whipping up the cream, so she got permission to escape the kitchen. She was eating wild blackberries in the meadow when a head poked around the bushes.

"Quill!" Lucy said, "I thought you were fishing!"

"Finished early!" Quill said, plucking a fat berry.

"Oh!" said Lucy. A lightning bolt struck as she realized Quill could replace Bekah as her ally. But then...Lucy couldn't picture her with the town ladies, and she didn't even want to think about combining her with Katherine again.

Quill looked at her closely. "What is it?"

"Um, nothing," Lucy fibbed.

"We're finished!" said Quill, popping another berry in her mouth. "Though I'll smell like smoked fish for a month now."

They sat down in the grass, pushing up their sleeves and hiking their skirts to their knees to get as much sun as possible on their legs. Lucy said, "I have a few minutes. Tell me about it?"

Quill told Lucy how they caught the fish, split it, and smoked it on rocks or hung strips over a wood frame, stretching the pieces to prevent raw pockets that would rot later. With a blush, she confessed that she'd wrecked a whole batch while thinking of William Brinnon. Lucy remembered the handsome young man from the barn dance and how he'd choked when Quill was mentioned. While Quill daydreamed, the salmon had burned to a crisp. The aunties scolded her silly, making her tend the fires another whole night. She was weary from lack of sleep.

Lucy was much more interested in the William part than the fish, but Quill went on quickly, "Best salmon run in twenty years! There's to be a potlatch, at Discovery Bay!" Her voice thrummed with excitement.

"So, you're busy today?" Lucy was ashamed at the relief that swept through her.

"Oh, yes! I'll be going back..." She stopped midstream and glanced around the clipped field, at the chairs and tables set out, "You having a gathering too?"

Lucy told her about the quilting bee. Quill laughed when Lucy said it would last all day.

"A potlatch lasts many days!" said Quill. She explained that people came from far away in large sea canoes, even from the top of Vancouver's Island.

"The people stealers?" Lucy asked, worried.

"Oh, no. They are far, far north! Beyond Vancouver's. These families are just across the water, on the tip of the island. We have cousins there."

Lucy was feeling put out by one of Quill's earlier comments. "Our party might be only for an afternoon," said Lucy, "but it's still important. Wait!" she thunked her forehead with the heel of her hand. "I almost forgot! Thank you for the baskets, on my birthday... for remembering me. And please," she added, "thank Henry."

Quill's dimples flashed. "He took forever! Could not decide on a gift for you." She put her finger up to her lips. "Don't tell him I said that. Swear!"

Lucy crossed her heart and swore, glad that Quill had told her. Then she grew warm, thinking of Henry choosing her gift.

"I will always remember you," said Quill, in an odd tone.

"I meant remember someone like you did, by giving a gift," Lucy said. "You don't need to *remember* me like one of us is leaving!" But Quill shook her head and left shortly after. Lucy wondered: Had Quill sensed her reluctance to invite her to the bee? Or was she thinking of something else? Perhaps she'd seen the newspaper, or heard the whispers in town.

Up in her room, Lucy propped her book open with her toe. She was nearing the end of *Hunchback* and couldn't resist getting in a few more pages while she changed into her party clothes. A fire raged in Paris and the gypsy girl who had befriended the hunchback was in danger. He hoped to save her, but the whole city distrusted the gypsies and the fire raged...

"Lucy?" her mother called. "Are you up there? What's taking you so long?"

She'd forgotten to lace up her boots, and had to stop and tie them before she tripped and fell headlong down the stairs. She caught a glimpse of herself in the hallway glass: new dress but not too fancy, clean hair, very dirty white boots. Out the window, she spied Katherine tromping across the grass.

Her mother called again, "I could use two more hands down here!" An edge of desperation in her voice brought Lucy to her senses. Reluctantly, Lucy joined her.

"Halloo," sounded from the porch. It was Ruby's mother, early. Lucy had never seen her before. She wore a hat piled high with a bird's nest and a bunch of long feathers. Anyone standing too close might get one up their nose.

"Oh my!" Lucy's mother murmured, stepping forward with a smile as she whispered, "Here we go!"

Katherine, Ruby, and a gaggle of younger sisters straggled behind Ruby's mother, all buried under a quilting hoop and baskets of fabric. *This is going to be about as much fun as having your teeth drilled,* thought Lucy. The girls would have walked right past her, if Ruby's mother hadn't stopped them, saying firmly, "I'm sure you'd like to see what Lucy does for fun?"

Sure they would, thought Lucy. The same thought was written on Katherine's face.

"Lucy?" her mother elbowed her in the side.

"Come see the chicken coop?" she offered.

"Chickens?" sneered Katherine. "I've seen those before."

But Ruby said, "I'd love to. I simply love animals!"

Lucy, who'd been ready to go inside, turned back. "Really?" She led the way around the corner of the house. Katherine stood still for a moment, as if thunderstruck, and then scuffed along behind them.

"Your garden's big!" complimented Ruby, as they walked past.

"Keep it all myself... *now,*" said Lucy. They exchanged a *You know what I mean* look.

"When *my* mama was expecting," said Ruby, who came from a family of eight, "I worked myself to a frazzle: ironing and carrying and boiling. Whew! I was worn out when those little babies arrived!"

"Don't I know it," agreed Lucy, "but I like working in the garden. I can hear the ocean out here, kind of like music."

"Music, my eye!" interrupted Katherine. "Didn't you hear about the *Anabelle Lee*? Foundered off Deception Gap. All thirty people lost. Music!" she muttered.

Ruby spoke up. "Honestly, Katie!" she said.

Lucy studied her from the side, wondering if she could see the backbone Ruby seemed to have grown overnight.

Katherine spat on the ground. "S' true! I swear it!"

"I think I heard the same," said Ruby. "But no one's going to wreck out there now. The water's calm as glass." She frowned. "Besides, it's bad luck to speak of death at a quilting."

Lucy stared. She'd never once heard Ruby, or anyone else, go up against Katherine.

"Never know how fast trouble will kick up," growled Katherine.

Lucy didn't know if she was describing it or planning it. Looking a little closer, she could see that Katherine's eyes were red, though her appearance was better than usual. She wore a clean apron over her dress and her hair was combed, but she'd definitely been crying. *I'll bet a hundred silver dollars it's Tate Altman.* Lucy imagined having to wake up to that face every morning, and go home to it every night, and shivered.

They'd reached the coop. "Meet Rhode Island Red," said Lucy. The girls laughed as the rooster squawked at them and flapped his red comb. "And Madame Belle." She pointed to the white chicken whose plumes were so fluffy, she looked as if she were wearing a ball gown.

"How pretty!" cooed Ruby. "Can I hold her?"

"Sure! I've tamed them," said Lucy, letting them into the coop.

Katherine looked skeptical, but Ruby scooped up Madame Belle and cradled her in her arms. Even Katherine seemed to find a friend in Rhode Island Red. She reached out and stroked his back a few times—quickly, as though she didn't want the others to see. Katherine grunted and said, "Best move before they poop on us."

"P'shaw!" said Ruby, brushing aside Katherine's comment. "Nobody ever died from a little chicken poo."

Lucy marveled again at Ruby's changed attitude, and marked it down to there being no boys in sight; or perhaps her mother had told Ruby to be friendly while visiting.

Or maybe, Lucy thought, *they're starting to like me?*

CHAPTER 21

Lunch, and What Happened After

Ruby's mother inspected the table they'd set on the porch. "Wonderful food, Amelia!" she said, as she loaded a double portion of every item onto her plate.

"A lot of it was Lucy," said her mother, putting an arm around her daughter's waist. "She's been a big help to me this summer!"

All the mothers smiled at Lucy.

"Nice to see a hard-working young lady," said Ruby's mother, frowning at her daughter. "Wish I had one!" All the goodwill drained out of Ruby's face, and Lucy groaned inside.

After lunch the older children chased the little ones and stuffed them with cookies until they got drowsy, then laid them down on quilts under the trees. Lucy ransacked her room for something to entertain the older girls. She pulled Dodger from his hiding place under her bed and put him in his basket. He'd grown so fat, he weighed as much as a full sack of flour. As she staggered downstairs, she could see the ladies under a big oak. Fabric flowed over their dresses, and their hoops were pulled tight over a section of quilt each. They spoke softly while needles flashed in and out. Every once in awhile, the breeze carried a comment about floss weight or stitch patterns to Lucy. When their voices dropped low, she knew they were sharing a thread of gossip. Her mother was smiling, and looked younger than she had in a long time.

Ruby and Katherine sat away from the others, near the edge of the woods. Lucy arrived out of breath, lugging the basket. She put it down, and before she could open it, Katherine said, "Injun baskets are a penny a dozen. But ohhhh, I forgot your precious Judge collects them." She spat, and then said, "Papa says they're full of vermin 'n should be burned."

"My father thinks something else entirely!" said Lucy, goaded into taking a high tone. "He's collecting them for the Smithsonian Institution."

"More like *your pa* belongs in an institution," jeered the girl.

Ruby broke in. "Katie, that's the worst thing you ever said! Don't you remember? That old teacher whipped you more times than you could count. Lucy's father is ever so much nicer. Take it back."

Katherine glared at Ruby. To Lucy's surprise, Ruby glared back. Lucy thought they might get into a fight right there on her lawn. Katherine seemed to deflate a little in the face of Ruby's resistance. She looked sideways at Lucy and said, "Um, well, I didn't mean your pa, Mr. Smith-so-nee-an," Katherine spit the "Smith" out like a bullet. "I meant that old boozer Swan. Do you know he lived with the Makahs? CRAAAZZZY!" she said, whirling her hand by her ear.

Lucy couldn't let it slip by, like she had that day by the trading post. "What makes you hate Indians so much?" she asked.

The girl's tanned face went oyster-shell white. She jutted out her chin and said, "Scared my ma off."

"Your father did, more likely!" Lucy was horrified to realize she'd spoken her thought.

Katherine's jaw clenched. "Take that back! They come along the swamp, hunting their birds. Scared my ma off. Sent her flying away." She tore at a threadbare patch in her skirt. "Me an' the little ones never saw no more of her—all 'cause of those Indians."

Lucy should stop, she knew, but Quill's family tended the bird nets down by Katherine's house, and she couldn't leave it alone. Not this time. She'd had her fill of backing down with Katherine. "Did they do something to her?" Lucy asked.

"No," muttered the girl.

"Well then, *what*?" demanded Lucy, putting her hands on her hips.

Katherine grumbled, and then her words swerved in a new direction. "You don't know what it's like, keeping the little ones fed, and papa happy." A haunted look came into her eyes. "Knowin' you might be dragged off to the orphanage, split from your sisters and brothers. Do you?" she shouted, and some of the ladies heads came up. "Miss Doted-on-by-Mama-and-Papa, you in your white boots. Miss I-Know-Everything."

Ruby sat with her mouth open, looking from one to the other of them.

"That's not fair," said Lucy.

"Little Miss quotes this and reads that, with all your books." She drew out the word *book* in a way that made Lucy know she was referring to the French book.

"The book," Lucy repeated.

"The book," Katherine repeated, with a sneer.

Lucy made a mighty effort to keep her temper. *Don't Don't Don't let her get to you!* she told herself. The book lay at the bottom of the bay, and Lucy was determined to leave it there.

"What book?" asked Ruby, frowning. "Katie, what did you do?"

"Miss Rich!" sneered Katherine. All three girls were on their feet now.

"I'm not!" Tears of anger choked Lucy's throat. She thought back to that first day on the cliff. All the words that had piled up since, like water behind a dam, seemed to flow out of her. "Look around you. I'm not rich! At least my father's not a drunk who terrifies his children, sells liquor to the Indians, and then blames them for his troubles!" Lucy grabbed Katherine's arm and pushed the sleeve up to reveal what everyone said was there: ugly purple and black bruises, some in the shape of fingerprints.

Katherine ripped her arm away and kicked the basket with a vicious WHACK!

Dodger shot out like lightening, leaping into the cover of the trees. Lucy ran after him. Then Katherine pelted after her, yelling,

"You take that back!" Then, as she began to catch up, "I'm gonna beat you up." Lucy knew she meant it, and ran faster.

Above her own pounding footsteps, the thud of Katherine's boots echoed in Lucy's ears, and farther away, the sound of mothers calling out. She was relieved to hear Katherine stumble. Lucy sped up, trying to keep Dodger in sight. The rabbit was fatter and slower than the first time she'd chased him. Lucy hoped to scoop him up and dive behind a tree before the girl caught up.

Just ahead, she heard a sound that made her heart stop: A whoosh, followed by a thud…the sound of an arrow hitting something soft, then a squeal and silence.

Lucy's steps slowed as she rounded the corner. There in the path lay Dodger, tipped over, with an arrow sticking out of his side. While she watched, the rabbit's legs twitched and then he was still. Her eyes filled with tears and her breath stopped in her chest. In a blur, Lucy saw Henry with a bow in his hand.

"Lucy?" he asked. He stood very still. Then he gently picked Dodger up, pulled the arrow out, and handed the limp animal to Lucy, who was gulping in air and trying not to let the sobs escape her throat.

"I didn't know," he said, touching her arm.

Katherine burst through the trees and rushed at them, her hand raised to strike. Before Lucy could even lift an arm to protect herself, Henry stepped forward and grabbed Katherine's arm, pinning it neatly behind her. The whole thing happened so quickly, and with so little noise from Henry, that Lucy wondered if she were in a dream. For a moment, she felt a surge of pure victory, but then she touched Dodger's fur and looked into Katherine's eyes. What she saw there was not trouble but raw fear. Henry had a grim look on his face. He twisted Katherine's arm tighter and the girl winced in pain, but she did not utter a sound.

"Stop! Henry, let her go." Looking through her tears, Lucy said, "Go home, Katherine. I don't want to see any more of you." She glared at the girl over her rabbit. No one moved. Lucy stood up and made herself as tall as possible. She said, "Let go, Henry!"

and to Katherine, "Get away from here, now!" and pointed toward the path to town.

Henry released her and Katherine hesitated for a moment; then stomped away, rubbing her arm and casting a resentful look back. The ladies were very close and their agitated voices reached them through the trees. "What's happened?" "Where's Lucy?" "Is everyone all right?" and, "Ruby said someone was shot. Call my husband, at once!" The last voice definitely belonged to the sheriff's wife. Then a calmer voice, Lucy's mother, "Let's wait and see what's happened, shall we?"

"Lu-cee, I am sorry, but I must go," said Henry, taking both her elbows in his hands. "I will tell Quill, and then find something for you," here he touched Dodger's body, "when I can." He touched her cheek, and was gone.

The next face Lucy saw was her mother's, down low. Lucy didn't even realize that she'd crouched down and buried her face in her rabbit's fur. Her mother laid a hand on Lucy's arm, then looked up saying, "What happened here? Where's Katherine?"

Lucy looked her mother in the eye and said, "I sent her away."

Her mother nodded, "And this?" She stroked the rabbit's head, then wiped blood from Lucy's face where it had lain on Dodger's body. She gave her a handkerchief for her eyes.

"It was that Indian boy," said one of the girls, "I saw him!" The ladies listened with alarmed expressions.

"Not Henry?" her mother asked.

"Mother!" hissed Lucy, "He didn't know it was Dodger."

Her mother thought for a moment. "That I'll grant you, but what was he thinking, hunting so near the house?"

Ruby stepped forward. "He attacked Katherine! I saw him!" she said.

"That's not true!" said Lucy. She stood with Dodger in her arms and glared at Ruby, who squirmed a little. "Henry was protecting me," Lucy insisted. She knew this would be very bad for him, if added to the list of things he'd been mixed up in. But no one seemed interested in listening to her version of the story.

The ladies made their way back to the house—passing the basket, which was broken in two on the spot where the argument had started. Lucy's mother settled her on her bed with a cold compress, and went back to her guests. The ladies had moved to the shade of the front porch, and their voices came in through Lucy's open window. If she hadn't been so unhappy, she would have laughed at the beehive buzz of conversation outside.

"That girl needs to be taught some manners!" said a voice.

"She's got no mother, the poor poppet."

Mrs. Blanc let out an unladylike snort. "Mother or no, Katherine's got a hateful streak."

"Just high spirits, I think." Ruby's mother.

High spirits? Was the woman a simpleton?

"Laura," Mrs. Blanc's voice was stern. "I know you were close to Katherine's mother, but you must see… ?" Part of the conversation was lost, but then, "father… criminal… better away from him."

Lucy opened the window wider. The ladies were directly below her. "Her mother asked me to keep an eye on them," said Ruby's mother, "and Lord knows I've tried to do my part."

"Well, you must do more," said Mrs. Blanc. "Take her in!"

"Take her in? Why, you can't mean it! There are five children in that house, and Katherine takes care of them. I'd have to take them all!"

"Yes, there are," said Mrs. Blanc in a soft voice. "Five young souls, in that place."

Lucy pulled the window closed, not wanting to hear any more about Katherine and her awful father. Out of habit, she reached under the bed for the comfort of her rabbit, forgetting that they'd left Dodger in the shed until her father could help bury him. A fresh bout of tears began, and a dull ache in her chest. She curled up on the bed, too weary to think.

Quill's voice echoed in her mind, "We always find room; we make room for others."

CHAPTER 22

Choices and Lies

The next morning, Lucy woke with a very clear mind. As she dressed, she felt the pieces of her plan click into place.

She found her mother downstairs, sunk into a chair with her feet propped up. Her face was the color of chalk. She tried to rise, but Lucy said, "No, Mother, you sit." One thing Lucy had to give her mother: she did not speak when silence was needed. She watched Lucy's face with concern, but didn't ask her any questions. Lucy was grateful; trying to talk about any of it would have restarted the tears.

Lucy couldn't leave her weary mother with all the chores, so she adjusted her plan. She rolled up her sleeves and fed the chickens (trying not to look at Dodger's corner of the pen), set the bread to rise (trying not to look at the stove where he'd hidden), swept the porch (trying not to look at the meadow where she'd chased him), and set a cold cloth on her mother's forehead. The sun was well up in the sky by the time she felt satisfied that there was nothing left to do.

Trying to sound normal, she asked, "May I go see Mrs. Blanc?"

Her mother's eyes searched Lucy's face. Then she swung her feet down and went to the kitchen to bundle up a napkin with left-over treats. For once, she didn't nag Lucy to tidy herself.

"You rest," said Lucy. "I'll ask Mrs. Blanc if I can stay for dinner, so you can have a little quiet." The lie sat badly with her, but she *did* want her mother to get some rest. She looked like she hadn't slept at all.

"I'll send your father after you later," said her mother, following her out to the porch with her heavy gait. She rested a hand on her large stomach. "But he might be busy right through 'til sunset, and I'm in no condition..."

"That would be fine!" Lucy said, and her mother looked at her more closely. "I mean, Mrs. Blanc and I have a lot of French to catch up on."

Lucy gave a little wave and ran across the meadow. She felt her mother's eyes on her as she hurried past the place where the argument had started. Lucy entered the trees and rounded the bend, trying not to look at the dark stain on the path, or think about the freshly disturbed dirt behind the chicken coop with a cross on top made from twigs. She paused to catch her breath.

Someone was approaching through the trees from the other side of the point, and by their grunts and loud breathing they were carrying something heavy. Lucy dived behind a tree.

"Did you hear someone?" a voice asked.

"What if I did? It's a free territory," someone answered. *Tate Altman!*

"Yeah, but what we're about to do ain't so lawful," said a third voice. The voice was oddly familiar, but Lucy couldn't place the speaker.

Altman laughed—an ugly laugh. *Just like his daughter's,* Lucy thought. But then, not. Now she'd seen the fear in Katherine's eyes, Lucy realized her feelings had begun to change. The girl would always be awful, but Lucy felt something like pity for anyone who had to live with that man.

"The fine upstanding people of town will thank us, once it's all done." Altman grunted, setting something down on the ground with a thump. There was no clinking sound, so Lucy didn't think this was a rum run. What was he up to?

"Long as it gives us time, for what we're doing," said a ragged voice. She didn't know for sure, but she guessed that might be the Indian with the scars.

"It worked out in Chimacum, didn't it?" Altman asked.

An answering grunt passed as agreement, and the men hoisted their burdens and moved on toward town. Lucy peered out and saw three backs: Altman's, the scarred Indian's and a third—the one who sounded familiar. But she couldn't identify him from the back. She was relieved not to see Henry.

Lucy blew out her breath. The men in town knew whatever it was Altman had planned, from their comments at the waterfront. But she didn't think the tribe did. Lucy thought they should know something was brewing. She headed toward the beach, feeling she had a good reason now for what she'd already planned to do.

She reached the lake, surrounded by its fringe of sweet peas and long grass. Quill and Henry's canoe was on the beach, alone. Lucy stepped in and lay down among some bulky packages, curling into a ball and pulling a blanket up over her.

The sun had barely reached midday. She had hours yet before her father would come looking for her at Mrs. Blanc's. All she had to do was wait, and hope Henry and Quill came soon, and didn't look too closely at the heavily packed canoe.

Lucy enjoyed the gentle rocking of her bed. *Rocking?* She'd fallen asleep! A voice had spoken—Quill's. The wool blanket tickled Lucy's nose and she told herself firmly not to sneeze. Another voice murmured, low and pleasant, accompanied by the slap of waves on the canoe. *So easy*, Lucy was thinking, when a sneeze exploded out of her.

"Aiyya!" yelled Quill, whisking the blanket away. Lucy tried to see in the glare of the sun. William held a paddle, raised to strike. Quill stood with the blanket in one hand, wide-eyed.

"Lucy!" Quill said. Her mouth gaped open.

William laughed and said, "I thought the canoe felt awful heavy!"

Lucy sat up, happy that they were surrounded by water. She hoped they were too far out for them to want to turn around and take her back. She quickly explained about Dodger and Katherine. She expected Quill's face to relax, but it didn't. As Lucy told them her plan, it didn't sound very impressive: getting away by hiding in a friend's canoe. She realized she hadn't thought much past the getting away part.

After a long silence, Quill said, "I thought you were a bundle for the Potlatch." She glared at Lucy. "You didn't ask! You'll bring trouble."

Lucy was speechless.

William held the paddle still above the water, looking from one girl to the other.

Quill sat down. "What if your mother goes out to look for you?" she asked.

"She thinks I'm at Mrs. Blanc's for supper."

"You lied to your mother?"

Lucy shifted uneasily in the bottom of the boat.

"Let her come for the games," said William. "That can't hurt anything." He worked on Quill with his smile and Lucy was reminded of her father with her mother. "I have to go back to town tonight. On the way home, I'll bring her back!" He started paddling again.

"William!" Quill protested, grabbing the paddle. "People in town are full of fear. What will happen when they find she's missing?" She looked over at Lucy. Quill rushed on. "They blame us for everything. Someone steals from a store? It's our fault. Someone takes whiskey? Our fault!" Her forehead creased. "They do not care which one of us makes trouble. They want an excuse to make all of us go."

"Where?" asked Lucy.

"To the reservation," said William. "The tribes signed a treaty seven years ago."

"What do you mean, 'the tribes'?" asked Quill. "You're part of this...of us!"

William looked uncomfortable and Lucy thought about his

position and Matthias'— having Indian mothers but living in homes built by settler fathers. William seemed to take part in the life of the tribe more than Matthias did, but he didn't live with them.

"It says we can still gather the fish, the berry, the cedar bark… in our old places," said Quill, "Which would be here!" She gestured over the water. "We're not farmers!" she said. "How are we to gather fish on dry land?"

William stared at Quill with a look Lucy couldn't interpret. She knew deep currents moved under the surface of the conversation, between William and Quill but also involving the Brinnons and Chimacum and the Bishops and the S'Klallam and Port Townsend. She and was afraid to say a single thing to add to the general complicatedness of things.

"Why don't you tell Lucy one of your stories?" William turned to Lucy. "Quill tells the best stories! I think she may be the story keeper one day. That is… " he drawled, "if she doesn't keep burning the fish."

Quill scooped seaweed out of the water and threw it at him, and William laughed.

"A story," said Lucy. "That would be good!"

William smiled at her and dipped his head in thanks. He pulled a half-smoked cigar out of his pocket and lit it, smoking and paddling while Quill considered. Lucy felt sure that his mother and father wouldn't be too happy if they saw him puffing away while he rowed two young women about.

When Quill settled herself to tell the story, Lucy knew she'd be allowed to go with them.

"My auntie tells me this one when there are many stars," Quill said, and began:

"*Once, there were two sisters ready to be getting a husband. On a lucky night, they saw two of the most brilliant stars up in the sky. 'Oh, my!' said the older sister, 'I wish that star could be my husband!' and pointed at the brightest star, which flashed with a golden light. Flash, flash it went, calling to the girl. The younger one said she would be happy with a smaller star, and picked one to the side, a little dimmer, yet still quite nice."*

"I like that girl!" said William, "Doesn't expect too much." Quill's glare shushed him.

"Next night, the girls went out again. Both stars were still there, calling to the two beautiful maidens. Suddenly, the two stars disappeared and two handsome young men appeared. They stole the girls' hearts and took them with them, up into the night sky."

Quill stopped for a moment, then said, "The dimmer star was especially fine looking... with black eyes."

William raised an eyebrow at Quill and Lucy noticed that he had green eyes. "You added that part!" he said.

"Keep going, please!" said Lucy, wondering if she'd hear the real story with all the banter between the storyteller and the paddler. Quill nodded and continued.

"Up in the sky, huge stones crashed together, and great fires flared. The girls had to be very quick to stay alive and not be crushed. They passed safely through these obstacles. But one night, they came to an opening in the heavens where they could see everything down on earth—all the ones they loved, and the forests and animals and rivers they knew. The girls were lonely for their own people and country, and tired of jumping around boulders and fires."

"So what did they do?: asked Lucy.

"Jumped into the fires from sadness and were burnt to a cinder!" said William.

Quill rolled her eyes. "Why did you ask for a story if you have no patience to listen?"

"They tied some cedar limbs together to make a long rope. The oldest slid all the way down, then she twirled the rope in a great circle to let her younger sister know it was her turn to come down. The younger one slipped down behind her, before the stars could find them. They landed in the middle of a prairie, and the rope is still there."

"Where?" asked Lucy.

"In the middle of Vancouver's Island."

"What about the star-husbands?" asked Lucy.

"I'll ask my great-uncle when he comes to the potlatch. He says the dimpled one was his grandfather, and that he longs for the stars because he is part star."

"Are you sure your great-uncle is part star?" asked William. "Maybe the girls just found more suitable husbands down here, more regular."

Looking at Quill, with the dimples in her cheeks and her eyes flashing, Lucy could believe there might be a sliver of star in her. She thought of Henry, with his quickness.

"Well," said Quill, "They say he cut holes in star shapes in the roof of his long house. It's like sleeping outside, inside. Even in the daytime the roof looks like the night sky, when the sun shines through the holes." She waved her hand overhead, as though the sky was really a cedar roof, with little pinpricks everywhere.

All at once, Lucy saw things differently. Far from being heavy and dark, as they'd seemed to Lucy, for Quill and her family the cedar plank houses and the forests with their low boughs and dense layers of needles were a covering that kept them close and safe, like a quilt.

CHAPTER 23

At the Potlatch Too Long

They landed at Discovery Bay, and Lucy felt a tug at her thoughts...something she needed to remember, but she was soon distracted. She hadn't thought much about her destination when she hid in the canoe, only that she could see Quill. She'd wanted more than anything to get away from town, but she'd forgotten about the potlatch. Rows of canoes and tents lined the sand, and flocks of children flitted about like seagulls, playing. She recognized several from their berry picking trip. Quill pointed out the huge seagoing canoes built for longer voyages. As they trudged up the sand, Lucy was glad to spot Henry down the beach. He lifted a hand above a crowd of young men and waved. She caught the flash of his smile.

"You know," Quill said in her ear, "Henry might be waving at William, or me."

Lucy's smile faded, but then she felt Quill's poke in her ribs. "Quill!" she said, embarrassed. Lucy was often caught off guard by the speed with which Quill could go from serious to joking, often without a change of voice or expression. It made Lucy feel slow, and sometimes even a little irritable. She wanted to join in, but the timing escaped her.

Gesturing toward a tent, Quill said, "Judge Swan is here."

"Judge Swan?" Lucy had hoped to slip back to her house without anyone knowing she'd been away. "That's a problem!"

"Maybe." Quill made a face. She lifted her hand in a bottle tipping motion.

"Ohhhh." Lucy nodded. "I see." Not good for the judge, but perhaps helpful for Lucy if she wanted to remain unseen.

The aunties were working midway up the beach, and glanced in their direction. Some looked at her quite intently. Lucy was afraid they'd respond the way Quill had. But they gave her bark tea in a chipped white mug, while the older aunties drank theirs out of clam shells. The tea soothed and warmed Lucy, as did the murmurs of conversation and laughter as the women worked around the fires that were placed all along the waterfront.

The auntie who'd helped wash Lucy's egg-stained pockets on the strawberry island gazed at her. Lucy asked Quill why she was staring. Had she done or said something wrong?

"Far from it!" said Quill. "She says she'll remember you as the girl who found a whole egg among the shells, and thinks you should have a name like this." Quill grinned. "Not to spoil it, but she thinks *Lucy* is too plain, that you need something more."

Lucy felt a warm flush of gratitude, and smiled at the woman. "Please say thank you. But also, my full name is Lucinda!"

"They call my uncle 'Duke of York'," said Quill. She turned to Lucy. "Do you think they honor with these names, 'Duke of York,' or 'Prince George'?"

"Ummm, no," Lucy admitted. She thought of the Prince of Wales in England, with his coaches and palaces. He was supposed to be a playboy, showing up all over the place with different women at his side. He had visited Boston only a few years before. Her father had said at the time that the fellow lacked a backbone—something that might be needed in a future king. Everything she knew of Chetzemoka made her think of him as a serious leader of his people.

"They say," said Quill, "That we give names as a—" she stumbled over the word, "—blessing." One of the younger aunties laughed at that, and spoke swiftly. Quill translated, "Sometimes we give no name at all!"

"What? No name?" Lucy said. "But, why?"

"When a child is born, their parents watch him or her for a time, trying to find just the right name for them. If they make trouble, they might not get a name for a long time." Lucy thought they might be pulling her leg. But the auntie next to Quill, who understood a fair amount of English, touched Lucy's arm and pointed at an angry looking youth by the water.

Quill nodded and said. "Oh yes! That one doesn't have a name yet, because his mother refuses to give him one." Lucy could see the reason written all over the stubborn looking face.

"How old is he?"

Quill asked the auntie. "Eighteen!" Then she gave Lucy a wry grin. "Your Katherine probably wouldn't get a name for, oh, ten years yet!" she said. Lucy laughed and felt better than she had since Dodger twitched and lay still. She understood that Quill was trying to cheer her up and apologize for her attitude in the canoe. Friends, she mused, were like that: a lot could be accomplished with one joke.

Lucy liked her new name. "Something Whole out of the Shells," something good in the middle of something broken: like Quill, and Henry, and Dodger. Her eyes filled with tears.

The aunties erupted with questions, which Quill translated. What had Quill said to make Lucy cry? Why had she upset their guest? While Quill explained about Dodger, two wrinkled hands came around Lucy's shoulders. She felt something soft settle on her and she was enfolded in a white blanket. Quill explained that the blanket was from Vancouver's Island, from a rare dog raised for their fine hair. "Very valuable! But the dogs are dying out, as everyone trades for Hudson's Bay blankets now." She waved her arm around the beach, "Some bring goods here to trade, while the waters are calm for crossing." She grinned. "Some come only to eat our clams!"

The aunties resumed their work of pounding roots with bone-handled tools. Lucy tried to help, but smashed her finger between the pestle and the rock, bringing fresh tears to her eyes. The aunties insisted she sit by the fire, which she did, looking into the flames and feeling useless.

Quill put hot rocks into a basket of water for cooking. All around them were baskets full of clams and salmon and herring, which the aunties shelled and gutted with little knives. She wondered where the men were, but figured they were in the long row of tents and log dwellings set above the high tide line. While the women worked, they sang a haunting tune that rose and fell. It seemed to catch the rising currents in the wind and echo off the hills behind them. A woman with a broad face and thick black braids led the singing. She looked strong and young, but her braids were threaded with silver. Her song had a strange, chilling, yet beautiful sound.

"She sings of the wind," said Quill. "It is her own song." Then Quill explained that the women of a family passed down their songs to their daughters. A song was a possession, and no one could sing someone else's without asking first. "My mother's song belonged to the chief's mother, my grandmother."

"Do you know how to sing it?" Lucy asked. "Is it yours now, or will it be given to you later?" It seemed a little like inheriting a mother's best silver, cedar hope chest, or a ring. A song wasn't a visible thing, but she understood the idea.

Shaking her head, Quill said, "Not yet. But soon, she will give me my mother's song." She nodded toward the woman who had led the singing. Lucy thought she saw tears in Quill's eyes. She hesitated, then put her arm around her friend's shoulders. Quill had never been one to hug, but she leaned into Lucy for a brief moment; then sat up again.

"Your aunties look worried," Lucy said, "or am I imagining that?"

"They have reason," said Quill. She stopped working for a minute, and then pounded her root with a fierce whack. "Once, a boy from our tribe worked as a guide for some bad white men. They yelled at him, spit on him, kicked him. He'd had enough. So, he cut their throats while they slept."

Lucy tried not to look as shocked as she felt. "Wh—what happened?"

"Soldiers came up from Fort Vancouver, on the Columbia River. Chetzemoka tried to hide the boy. He asked the soldiers to let us deal with him in our own way. We have justice here."

"Did they?"

Quill pounded harder, smashing the root. "The soldiers fired on the whole village, killing many of us—old ones, mothers, children, those who had nothing to do with the boy." She looked across the beach full of celebrating people. After a minute, she continued, "Now, the chief will not hide anyone. He can do nothing to protect a S'Klallam who upsets the settlers." Quill looked down the beach toward Henry.

"Even his own family?" asked Lucy.

Quill nodded. "Even his own nephew."

CHAPTER 24

Danger Awaits

The air cooled and the light started to fade. The world drew in close around the beach, the cove, and the dark blue sky.

"Time for games," said Quill.

"Games?" Lucy asked. They'd been helping prepare food for a long time. She'd thought they'd be leaving soon to arrive home by late afternoon, like all their other outings. But she hadn't taken the potlatch into account. Her father would be knocking at Mrs. Blanc's door any moment. She grabbed Quill's hand. "It's getting very late!"

Quill dragged Lucy forward. "First, Henry must pull. You'll see!" She looked at the sun. "Anyway, you could never have made it in time. I thought you must know that when you came."

Lucy was tempted to grab a boat and row herself home, but she knew she'd hardly make it out of the bay before she capsized, much less all the way back. She turned her attention to the beach, trying to distract herself, and tried to make sense of what was happening.

A mass of swirling bodies had split into two groups. On one side Henry's family gathered, including his uncle George, William, and a man Lucy didn't know. All had rolled up their shirt sleeves, and those wearing shoes had taken them off, gripping the sand with their toes.

"Who is that man?" Lucy pointed at the one with a web of fine scars on his face.

"That," said Quill in a level voice, "is my father."

"Your father?" Lucy wished her voice would quit squeaking.

Quill never spoke of her father and Lucy had never thought to ask about him. He stood at the head of the team, and his intense look reminded her of Henry. Quill told Lucy their team had rarely been beaten.

A short but thick rope divided the two groups for tug-of-war. The captains both grabbed an end and held on tight. Each team member held onto the man in front of him, making a long chain. With a loud shout, the tug-of-war started. Muscles bulged, sinews stuck out. The men sweated and strained while the crowd pressed in, calling loudly to urge on their side. But the rope did not move.

At last, the opposing team managed to gain a few steps. They began to look hopeful. But just when they seemed to be winning, Quill's father nodded his head and the S'Klallam team moved as one. They gave a giant heave, pulling the the rope and the other team back over the line, and the losers collapsed like a house of cards. Moans came up from the men on the sand, and the winning team lifted their captain and ran around the beach with him.

Everyone crowded in to congratulate the winners, and Quill pulled her father out of the mass. "Father, this is Lucy," she said, then spoke in S'Klallam. He was tall up close, but he had that slender grace Lucy saw in Henry.

Lucy dropped a curtsy and Quill's father dipped his chin in reply.

"He lives in the hills, and doesn't see people often," said Quill. "He doesn't know much English." Her father spoke slowly, giving Quill time to translate. "He says that I speak often about our lessons, and thanks you for teaching me." His eyes remained steady on Lucy's face while Quill spoke the words in English.

Lucy stuttered out, "N-no, well, I don't, not really. She doesn't need one, that is."

After Quill finished translating, he spoke to Lucy directly. "I thank you." He bowed. Quill said, "Your father is the one he wishes to thank the most."

Lucy dropped another curtsy and said, "I will tell him."

A hint of a dimple appeared in his one smooth cheek, making her wonder if he'd been as handsome as his son when he was younger. Her eyes widened as she admitted to herself that Henry was the handsomest boy she knew. Quill's father wore a puzzled expression.

"Lucy?" asked Quill.

Lucy realized she was staring at the scars on his face and arm. *Don't look—not at the scars—look anywhere else, no not in his eyes, that's too bold.* She gave up and dropped her gaze. When she looked up, he was smiling at her. Lucy sensed that he liked young people very much and wondered why he didn't come down from the hills more often.

"Why did you stare at my father like that?" asked Quill, as he left.

Lucy flushed, not about to tell her the Henry part. "Where did he get that scar?"

"A bear. He came between a mother and her cubs."

"Goodness! Did he kill her?"

"No," Quill said. "We think she gave him the bear spirit. He's the best hunter here." Quill's voice revealed her pride.

"But his arm?"

"You cannot argue with a bear and come away smooth!" She grimaced. "They say it was in shreds! My mother was the one who put nettles on the wound, and the white mud of the healers. Then he mended, and took her for his wife."

Lucy thought enviously of the gifts in Quill's family: the hunters and healers, the wrestlers, singers and weavers, with stars in their roofs and a way with seals. In her own family? A quilter, some teachers, and her father in his spectacles adding columns of numbers or preparing lessons.

Lucy laughed. "I can't see *my* father wrestling a bear. A sentence maybe, but not a bear."

Quill frowned. "Your father was the same, when he stood before those men." She pointed to the mill. "He was strong and he kept Henry safe, and me. That is why my father thanks you."

"Oh, I see!" said Lucy, wishing yet again that she'd stood up for Quill at the Trading Post. Then she might be famous in the tribe for more than a few bird's eggs.

There was a hullabaloo, and they turned to watch the older boys tearing down the beach with sand flying up behind them. Henry won the race by a large margin, and Lucy was surprised to see him jump up and down like one of the first graders in the schoolyard. He glanced the girls' way to see if they were watching. Lucy couldn't help smiling at the joy flooding his face.

The sun slipped down to the horizon behind the boys, a liquid ball melting and flattening as it rested on the water's edge. Lucy's worries grew even as the light dimmed and a breeze rose. "I must go!" she said, but Quill had split off to talk with William. While the two whispered together, Lucy thought about the voice she'd heard that day. Now that she was standing on the beach at the same bay, she suddenly made the connection. Lucy remembered where she'd heard the voice of the third man in the forest before.

"Quill!" Lucy said. "We have to get back to town. Now!" But Quill shook her off, seeming content to remain right where she was, with William. Lucy had noticed this difference in their sense of time before. Quill and Henry rarely seemed to follow the demands of a clock. She knew they responded to the tides, the seasons, and the flow of fish, but she suspected that the word "hurry" did not exist in the S'Klallam language. She sat down hard on a log, and dropped her head into her hands.

When Henry passed by, he took one look at Lucy and asked. "What's wrong?"

Lucy looked up. "I need to get home," she said.

Before she could say more, Henry acted. He gathered William, Quill and his paddle, and moved toward their canoe. Lucy felt relief well up in her, and affection.

"Wait!" Lucy ran back to the auntie who'd wrapped her up, offering the blanket. The auntie shook her head and refused to take the blanket back. Lucy extended it again.

"Oh, please," she said. "This is too valuable for me. You only have a few, and I don't need it." She looked about frantically. "I'll take a basket! I love those." She pointed at one of the waterproof clam baskets by the fire. But the woman set her chin and shook her head *no* again.

"She saw your face when you held it," said Quill, who'd joined them. "It's obvious that you love it." The woman pressed the blanket back into Lucy's arms. "She will think of you using the blanket, and she will be happy," said Quill. "The more valuable the gift, the greater the honor to the giver. That is potlatch: gaining by giving away."

Lucy folded the lovely blanket against her and thanked the woman, telling her she would take good care of the treasure. But she still felt badly. How would the auntie stay warm now?

William and Henry paddled the canoe, with Quill and Lucy in the middle, but there was nothing cozy about this trip. As they pulled out into the wind, Lucy felt a cramp in her stomach. They must know she was gone by now. Would her father search the town first? What about her mother? Lucy imagined her trying to hurry down the stairway to the waterfront, awkward with the huge bump in her middle. What if she couldn't see, and slipped? And then those men she'd overheard, planning to do something "like Chimacum." Chimacum, she knew now, meant fire. Lucy groaned.

"We'll have you home soon," said William.

At the other end of the canoe, Henry looked relaxed after his evening of games. She envied him his calm. A shiver that Ruby would call "a goose walking over your grave" made the hair stand up on Lucy's forearms. She had a bad feeling about Henry's future in town.

"That man Henry hit with the knife," Lucy said, "He was in the woods, this morning!" She told them what she'd seen and heard. William and Henry exchanged a look.

Quill glared at them. "What do the two of you know about it?

Under Quill's anger, Lucy sensed worry. "Well, we can't do anything right this moment," Lucy said. "Tell me about your father?" Henry gave her a grateful smile, and Lucy promptly flushed to the roots of her hair. *At least*, she thought, *he's here*. If he were part of Altman's plans, Henry would be there with him in town and not at the potlatch.

Altman would probably set things in motion soon, with night falling.

After a while, Quill spoke. "My father is the tribe's hunter," she said. "He brings the oil for the potlatch fires, which is why he's here now." Lucy had pictured most Indians as hunters and said so. Quill shook her head. "Maybe in the mountains, or on the plains. But only a few S'Klallam need to hunt. The sea offers plenty of food," said Quill. Then she fell silent again.

Lucy dared a question. "Does your father have a... a woman?"

Quill wrapped her arms around her knees, but she didn't seem offended. "My father is not like others. He holds my mother's memory inside him, so there is no room for another."

Then why doesn't he try and find out what happened to her? Lucy wondered, but she clamped her lips tight shut to keep the thought inside.

Quill continued, "When my mother was alive he fished, but he does not like to be here... now." The wind whistled over the water and waves slapped the side of the canoe. Lucy pulled the white blanket close, thankful for its glow against the steely waves and the gathering night.

They drew near the sandy beach where the twins kept their canoe and where Lucy had first met them.

Lucy shook Quill, who was dozing. "Quill, look!" Torches blazed over the hill toward the beach, sparking flashes of metal from uniforms and guns.

"Soldiers!" said Henry, and swore.

CHAPTER 25

Wave Tossed

William cursed under his breath and pulled hard, first to slow their forward motion, and then to back the canoe away from the beach. Lucy bent over with the others to make the lowest profile possible, and hoped the soldier's eyes were blinded by torchlight. The boys paddled over the side, turning toward the shadowy bulk of Point Wilson.

Lucy's mind whirled. Was the man from the mill stirring up trouble? Something serious must be going on for the soldiers to be called out from the Fort. Her stomach clenched. Were they out searching for her?

They finally left the torches and soldiers behind, but as the canoe neared the point the night howled at them. Lucy recalled her father's tales—of ships wrecking as they tried to find their way past on wicked nights. She understood better now why the Indians beached their canoes and walked across land to town. She gripped the side as the boat shivered with the impact of the waves, and peered into the dark. She tried to make out the headland, and the trees that sheltered her house. Nothing but cliffs and water on this side, and soldiers. The boys would have to work their way out into open water and around to reach the beach below her house on the other side.

Slowly, they neared Point Wilson, working their way along the outer side of corner of land that marked the mouth of the straits. The cliffs of Whidbey Island jutted out from the opposite side to form the other part of the mouth, invisible in the dark. Turbulent water surged back and forth between the two headlands, with the water and winds clashing at the intersection of straights and sound, and the waves churning crazily. The wind struck like a hand pushing them sideways, and they almost capsized. Saltwater sloshed into the boat. Henry and William fought to bring the nose of the canoe around and head out farther, so they wouldn't be pushed onto the rocks at the base of the cliffs. Lucy blessed the rising moon that lit their way as the boys yelled directions to each other, their voices snatched away by the wind.

They paddled fiercely, first pushed toward shore and then fighting their way out again, always about to be dashed at the base of the cliffs. Each time they lined up with the same spot: the white roots of a huge snag that had been washed up.

They were making no progress.

Lucy felt seasick. She was soaked clear through, even with the white blanket. She made herself stop looking at the snag on the shore and prayed for protection. She recalled a conversation she'd had with Quill. It felt like a hundred years ago, but was only the day before. Henry had found a guardian spirit, Quill had told her. Lucy had felt a little uncomfortable, wondering if she was betraying her faith to be discussing such things, but she was curious.

"How do you get a guardian spirit?" Lucy asked now. "How did Henry?"

Quill didn't answer for awhile. Lucy had never seen her anxious in a canoe before, but with each jolt of the boat against a wave, an answering quiver went through Quill's body. Her hand gripped the edge of the canoe. The boys fought to turn the prow again, so they'd take the waves head-on. After awhile, they'd moved out far enough for the boat to settle into a better rhythm.

"Henry went into the mountains while we were fishing." Quill said, leaning in close so Lucy could hear. "I say he wanted to run away from gutting fish, but he says he was called to go and found something. I think maybe he did."

Lucy agreed. Henry seemed more at peace. "What do you think he found?"

"It's not something we talk about, usually," Quill said. "But since we may not survive the night, I will tell you. I think he dreamed of the sun. The sun often chooses orphans: a great spirit, helping those who lose their way." Her eyes rested on Lucy. "Do you have a guardian spirit?"

Lucy hesitated, unsure. "God's spirit is always with us."

Quill asked, "Is it one Great Spirit or many?"

Lucy got tangled in her own words. "It's one, but also three. Spirit and Jesus and God. All the same, but not." Lucy thought for a moment. "He is himself."

Quill didn't seem particularly troubled by the complications of the Trinity. "And does this spirit watch over you and help you?" she asked.

"Yes!" said Lucy, suddenly sure. She'd never thought much about the faith her parents passed down to her. Now, in the middle of the waves, with water filling the bottom of the boat, she felt protected—surrounded inside her soul, like the white blanket around her body. As if the little craft were being held, cradled in the midst of the waves.

The canoe struggled against the forces of wind and water. Lucy couldn't help thinking, *Mrs. Blanc's husband must have perished on a night like this.* When Quill glared at her, she realized she'd spoken aloud and put a hand up to her mouth. "Oops, sorry!" she said.

Then, inch by inch, they started to make progress around the point—still pushed toward land, or suddenly rocked by a rogue wave, but moving forward. Once around the tip, the currents lined up in one direction and the fiercest winds were blocked by the bulk of land. They could catch their breath. The canoe floated free, resting on the gentler swells, and the boys sagged over their paddles, breathing hard.

"Ho!" called William, grinning at Henry. "No one's made it around that point in a long while! At least, not on a night like this." He raised his paddle over his head with both hands and let out a whoop and a yell. "Victory!"

They all expected Quill to tease, but she exhaled in one long groan, "Aiyyy!" They turned toward the glow that was reflected in her eyes.

Huge fingers of flame licked and roared, soaring into the night sky over one end of Port Townsend, over Quill's home at Kah Tai. The whole village was on fire.

"Henry?" Quill whispered after awhile. Her twin didn't answer but his body, which had been puffed with triumph moments before, deflated.

A horrified look crossed William's face. "Were all the old aunties out?"

"Yes," Quill said. "All at the potlatch."

Lucy was glad no poor soul was trapped inside. They had drifted closer to that end of town while they watched. The houses looked like giant match sticks, lined up and blazing above the beach. While she watched, one of the bird nets caught and singed like a strand of hair held over a flame. She could see its burning bits floating up into the sky. They'd be like traveling tinder for anything they landed on. "They'll call out the firemen," she stuttered, "You'll see. They'll get the brigade out. My father will help, surely! Someone will..."

"Do you think so?" asked Henry, his voice hollow.

"Our homes!" Quill wailed.

"The other S'Klallam—they'll take you in!" said Lucy. "Remember, 'always room'?"

"Enough for a few more," said Quill, looking at her wild-eyed, "but a whole village?"

They had been floating aimlessly. For some reason, Lucy imagined her mother's jar of preserves on a shelf in one of the houses, exploding from the heat.

Lucy didn't know how long they sat drifting before a bell started clanging. "Maybe now?" she asked.

"Ha!" said Henry. He pointed.

Handing water from man to man, a bucket brigade was wetting down the trading post and other businesses at the end of town closest to the fire. But no one seemed to be moving around the Indian village.

"The village…it's past saving," said William.

Henry jabbed his paddle into the water, aiming toward the fire. William lunged across the girls and grabbed his hands. "Not this time, cousin," said William, and the two of them locked eyes over the top of the paddle. William continued, "The soldiers are here! Remember? They'll scoop you up…or worse."

"We have to do something!" Henry said, pulling to try and free the paddle. He shouted into William's face. "Or are you afraid? Too busy being safe to help anyone else?"

William pulled his right arm back to punch Henry.

"Please, don't," Quill pleaded, grabbing Will's fist.

Lucy wasn't sure if Quill was pleading with the boys, the town, or the fire. The voices she'd heard around town echoed in Lucy's head: "clear out that eyesore down by the water," and "move those Indians onto their reservation, once and for all." Altman must have been talking about the fire in the woods that morning. But why would he risk it, with his own home so close?

"We don't want to be seen," said William, sitting back down. With the moon rising through a gap in the clouds, their canoe would stand out against the glimmering waves. "We need to get back to Lucy's beach, but I'm too tired to go a stroke farther," he said, and turned the boat toward the end of town farthest from the fire. Henry hesitated, then joined him.

Out of the Frying Pan

William angled the boat towards an empty dock and they bumped up against a piling. Close in, the bulk of the cliff blocked their view of the fire. There didn't seem to be a soul around, and all the ships were gone. Without its border of prickly masts, Port Townsend looked naked, even by night. Henry grabbed onto the dock.

"They must have moved the ships to a more protected spot, in case the whole town went up," said William, disturbing the dead silence. No one said anything in reply.

Lucy unfolded herself and stood up. Her head and shoulders rose above the planking of the dock. She wished she were a boy in pants, to make the scramble up and over easier. She placed her hands on the boards.

"Henry and I need to rest before we pull back to your beach," said William.

"Pull back?" asked Lucy, desperate to get out of the canoe and walk home on dry land. "I thought we'd walk!" She might never want to step into a canoe again, once she left this one.

"Back?" said Henry, at the same time.

"It's not safe here, especially for you!" said William.

"We should stop arguing and go get help!" said Lucy.

"For what?" asked Quill, rounding on her. "There's nothing left to help." Then Quill said something else.

"What?" Lucy asked, leaning in close to Quill. "I couldn't hear you."

"Your mother needs you," Quill said, in a flat voice.

"You don't need to tell me that!" said Lucy, but what she really felt was that Quill wanted to get rid of her. She'd felt that way all day.

"Of course her mother needs Lucy," said William, "but she needs her in one piece! After that, we'll see what can be done about the rest of it. The safest way to get her home is by boat." Lucy had a feeling that William was using her as an excuse to keep Henry away from trouble.

"It's too quiet," Henry said. "Strange."

Lucy agreed with him. Not one of the hotels and bars showed a flicker of candle or lamplight in their windows.

"I bet they're all out watching," said Quill.

Lucy hated to admit it but everyone loved a tragedy, especially a fire. The glow of flames stained the sky a bruised red over the ridge, the color of mud mixed with blood. *The color of war*, Lucy thought. She shivered, remembering the descriptions of recent battlefields: the gore from shattered men, and flags drowned in blood and muck—the war back east. Her mother had hoped they would find more peace out west.

The fire might be an accident, *possibly*. After the wet spring, everything had suddenly dried to a crisp. She didn't know for certain if Altman had set it. But this morning in the woods he had mentioned a distraction... For what? With the moon rising, the town was somewhat lit, but not enough to see into alleyways. The dock area was visible, and the road just beyond. Lucy mulled Altman's words from earlier that day. What were Altman, the logger, and the Indian with the scar planning to do while the town coped with the fire?

Time seemed to have stalled, though only a few minutes had passed. Lucy unpinned the small watch from her dress and put it up to her ear to hear its reassuring tick. A thud and the echo of a voice sent a shiver up her neck. "Hey!" she said, "There's something going on over there!"

A furtive movement on the porch of one of the hotels was

followed by the sound of breaking glass, and the thump of a door closing. "Look! By the stairs!" said Henry in her ear. Lucy could see a pool of inky black at the base of the stairs to uptown. Did she spy movement?

"I know who that is," he said, and the next moment he was up on the dock. William let out a string of curses and grabbed at Henry's foot, but missed. "Henry, wait, you idiot!"

Quill loosed a stream of rapid-fire S'Klallam at her brother's retreating form.

The clink of boots and gear from the direction of the fire turned them toward the other end of town. A group of soldiers was slowly working their way toward them, their torches flickering in and out as they passed behind buildings and checked doors and windows. When Lucy turned back, the dark had swallowed Henry.

"They're looking for looters," said William. "Smart!" His tone turned to dread. "Looters are shot on sight! They'll think Henry's one." He grabbed the planking.

"Oh no, not you too!" said Quill, as William launched himself up onto the dock and crouched there. "I'm just going to the corner, to keep an eye out," he said. "We may have to leave in a hurry, be ready!" In a blink, he was hidden in the shadows.

The words that poured out of Quill's mouth added heat to the air around them as she grasped one of the paddles and sat down.

Lucy stepped sideways, trying to see. The canoe rocked crazily and she clung to the boards, feeling the pitch stick to her clothes. Quill yanked her down, and Lucy uttered an unladylike word she'd never used before, and stood up again.

She was entirely unprepared for Quill's laugh. "You've never said that word before!"

Glass shattered somewhere nearby. By now both of them were up and pressed against the pier. If she made it to morning, Lucy knew she would recall the scent of pitch with the images of this night: burning skies, ash on the tongue, and blood—the blood where she bit her cheek and the blood that would come, which tasted like copper and smelled like dirt.

They couldn't see William, the soldiers or Henry, or whoever had made the noises. Only an empty pier bathed in moonlight, which was oddly like a wooden stage, lit up and waiting for the actors to step forward.

"I can't see," Quill whispered, flapping her hands in a helpless gesture so unlike her that Lucy trapped one in her own. *Was this all she and Quill could do? Hold hands and try not to panic?*

Suddenly they heard shouts, then shots.

Footfalls echoed from the right. William's head poked out of the shadows, craning around the edge of a building, then disappeared again.

"Like Chimacum," said Quill with a sigh.

"What do you mean?" Lucy asked.

"Altman set that fire at Chimacum. William told me."

"What about Henry?" Lucy asked.

"Always so stupid!"

"Tell me Quill. He didn't help, did he?"

In a bitter voice Quill said, "He follows."

"But, he didn't set the fire in Chimacum?" Lucy asked. "He couldn't burn someone's home, could he?"

Quill let out a deep sigh. "He was there, but he left. I don't know any more." She looked sideways at Lucy. "I didn't think he would—set fire to someone's house. But now, I don't know." She shook her head. "He doesn't seem like the same person anymore. Although he seemed better these past weeks. I don't know!" she repeated.

Before Quill could continue, a shadow darted from a doorway up the street. Henry! He padded onto the dock in a crouch. Lucy felt her heart leap at seeing him unharmed, but Will was nowhere to be seen. Henry had made it halfway down the dock when a voice rang out from the shadows. "You there, stop!"

Lucy hadn't thought she could be more worried, but she knew that voice and it brought ugly things to mind: red marks on arms and animals gutted in the forest. Quill pulled her down lower so they couldn't be seen, and the two of them peered over the edge.

Henry kept moving forward, but slowed.

"Hey!" Altman called. "Whoever you are—Flatface! Stop!"

Henry froze. "You never could tell me from any other Indian, day or night," he yelled back. His voice was flippant, but his body seemed tight as a piano wire.

"Got a boat here, *partner?*" Altman appeared at the base of the dock.

Partner? Lucy thought, her heart sinking.

Another figure appeared behind Altman. Lucy felt sure he was the scarred Indian. Both advanced on Henry, who faced them while backing toward the end of the pier.

"We should help!" whispered Lucy.

"No!" hissed Quill. "We have to be ready to get away."

"Damn you," Altman said. "Stop! You owe me." He kept on toward Henry.

Henry had his hands out. His head swiveled from Altman to the scarred Indian and back again. Lucy groaned when she spied the third robber climbing out of a second story window of one of the storehouses nearby. She guessed he must be the logger.

"Where is William?" she whispered, just as a figure burst out of the shadows and tackled the Indian. Quill gasped. Henry launched himself at Altman, and Lucy spied two things that made her heart drop into the cold waters beneath her: a knife in the scarred Indian's hand, and a gun in Altman's.

For a moment it seemed as though the scene had been frozen onto a glass photo plate: flames in the sky, the darkened buildings hunched to the left and right of the pier, the roadway lit by the rising moon. In front of it all, the dock with two pairs of struggling figures. She wondered briefly where the third man had gone.

Suddenly, there were soldiers everywhere: on the dock, in the alleyway, and more rushing from the direction of the fire. The crack of a shot echoed across the waterfront and off the cliff. Lucy and Quill crouched down in the canoe with their arms over their heads.

Someone was creeping toward them, but Lucy could barely hear for the blood pounding in her ears. She hoped to see Henry's face, but a moment later William slid over the side, one hand gripping the dock, and fell into the boat with a grunt.

"Go!" he said, through clenched teeth, holding one arm against his side.

"But… Henry?" asked Lucy. Quill started to push off and Lucy couldn't help standing up to look. Altman lurched toward her, with Henry holding onto him by his shirt.

"Wait!" Lucy said, staring into Henry's frightened face. He shook his head. "No!"

"Go!" said William.

Lucy sat down and grabbed a paddle. The more she tried to help, the worse things got. Quill said, "Stop!" They hadn't yet moved even two feet beyond the pier.

William sat in the center of the boat. Even in the dim light, Lucy could see the wet mark spreading on his coat, and a dark substance coating his hand.

As Quill pulled away, Lucy heard a voice up the street yelling, "Reinforcements! We need more men!" When they'd moved out a bit, they could see everything: A staggered line of soldiers approached, and another clump waited at the base of the pier. Her heart leapt into her throat when she spied a still shape on the dock. But Henry had thrown his arms around Altman's legs, and thrashed like a fish as Altman dragged him forward.

Quill jabbed again and again with the paddle while Lucy stared, mesmerized, at the glint of moonlight on steel in Altman's hand. When she caught his crazed stare, she shut her eyes tight.

"Flip him!" yelled Will. "Push him in!"

"Would you look at that," said Quill after a moment. Lucy opened one eye, then both.

Somehow Henry had broken free and was running up the hill. A group of soldiers moved off after him. The rest had split into two groups, with one set turning toward the warehouse window, and the others toward Altman. One figure still lay in the middle of the dock.

CHAPTER 27

Cries in the Night

Once clear of the harbor, Quill stopped paddling. "We need to bandage that," she said to William.

Lucy started ripping strips from her petticoat, glad for a job to do.

"Steady the canoe!" Quill said, thrusting the paddle at Lucy, but Lucy pushed it back at her. "I can handle this, and I can't steer the canoe!" Quill paused, then resumed paddling.

"He just winged me," the boy said, but there was too much blood for "just winged."

"Sit still!" she ordered, gently pushing him back onto one of the rough trading blankets.

Will gasped in pain, but said nothing.

Lucy could feel Quill's eyes on her as she unwound the white blanket from her own shoulders and covered him with it, missing its protection as the wind cut through her. Her stomach twisted at the sound he made when she reached under his coat and pressed the folded strips of petticoat against the wound to suppress the sticky flow. The pad was soon saturated with blood. Lucy had Quill fold another for her, throwing the first over the side. It blew back into the canoe and she tried not to think of the blood soaking into the water around her feet.

Blood, fire, death on the dock. She hoped against hope that Henry wasn't lying on a muddy street somewhere, bleeding. She shook her head and focused on William.

Quill paddled hard against a wind that kept gusting and shifting.

Every time she paused to catch her breath, they drifted back in the direction of town. Lucy did not like the grim set of her friend's shoulders. She wasn't doing much better with William's wound. She had to work hard to keep enough pressure to stop the blood, but not to hurt him, especially when the canoe lurched with a wave. When she'd finally stopped the flow of blood, she sat quietly next to him and watched her friend. Quill paddled with a smooth skill that surprised Lucy, as the boys always paddled when they traveled together. She envied Quill for having something to do.

The trip seemed to go on forever. William started to shake and Lucy tried to protect him from the water that lifted off the waves and slapped them in the face. Every few minutes, the night was punctuated by the report of a shot—some quite close. As trouble drew near her home from both sides of the point, Lucy prayed that her mother was not in the house alone.

As they moved into the shallows near Lucy's beach, they were greeted by an odd sight—an eerie light glowing up through the water, shifting and moving. Quill and Lucy jumped out, and the lights swirled away from them. They dragged the canoe up far enough so William could step out onto dry land, and Quill supported him up the beach. He called back, "The lights bring good luck! Scoop some into your hands and make a wish for Henry."

"Phosphorescence." said Quill as she moved away, making Lucy laugh for the first time in hours. Where had she learned that word?

One of the paddles had fallen into the water. Lucy chased it down and then stooped to catch the greenish motes. They pulsed in her palms and then faded, leaving faint trails of light like shooting stars. *But what wish?* Their glow reminded her of evening at the potlatch. When news of the fire reached them, the guests would scatter as sparks fly when a fire is struck, the embers fading as they float away in the dark.

She knew what her wish should be: that Henry would be safe, even if it meant leaving Port Townsend. She had a hard time forcing the whisper past her lips. She thought of Esmeralda the beautiful gypsy in her book, like a colorful moth that the hunchback rescued. He'd wanted to protect her up in the cathedral, but the gypsy girl hated being trapped inside. He'd had to release her to life outside, but her wings had burned.

How like Esmeralda Henry was, unable to resist the flicker of danger. And Icarus, the namesake of the ship, who'd soared too near the sun and melted his wax wings—plummeting to earth. Back in Boston, the myths lived in books with colorful plates, the orange flames safely printed. But here, the flames were real.

Trailing behind Quill and William, Lucy moved through the dark toward the hill above them. *Mother must be terrified, knowing I'm out in the middle of all this.* She found the path and climbed toward her house, ready to face whatever awaited her if only she could arrive home safe.

As they worked their way uphill, Lucy looked back. She imagined the scene in town—the dance of silhouettes darting in and out of the shadows, against the flicker of flames. She wished a wave would rise up and wash over the fire, over the whispers and rumors and all that burned behind the polite smiles in town. She wished everything could be washed clean.

Light glowed from every window of Lucy's house, warming the steps and the grass beyond. She ran past Quill and William and up the steps. As she reached the porch, the crack of a shot sounded somewhere in the woods nearby.

"Hurry!" Mrs. Blanc stood in the door, gesturing for them to get inside.

"Where's Mother?" Lucy asked.

Mrs. Blanc shook her head and pushed the door closed behind them. "Wait a minute," she said, putting a finger to her lips.

What did that head shake mean? "Where's Father? Is he here?" Lucy asked.

Mrs. Blanc's eyes fell on William. "What's happened?" she asked, and led him into the light of the parlor. Before anyone could answer her, they heard a moan.

"Is that mother? Is she all right?" Lucy asked.

"I need to check her," said, Mrs. Blanc in a reassuring voice. Lucy crept down the hall after her, to the door of her parents' room. Mrs. Blanc passed through and pulled the door closed, but not before Lucy caught a glimpse of her mother's chalk-white face, knotted with pain. She looked at Lucy, but didn't seem to see her.

Mrs. Blanc stepped out and pulled the door closed. "She's much easier, knowing you're home." She propelled Lucy down the hall with a firm push and said, "She says she'll see you soon, sweetie."

"Did she, truly?" Lucy asked. Her mother hadn't looked capable of speech.

Mrs. Blanc's hand flew up as though to slap Lucy, and they both froze.

Lucy's fingers flew to her mouth. "Oh, Mrs. Blanc! I wasn't— I'm sorry, I didn't mean to question you." She stared in horror at the woman who'd done more than any other to help her family. A hiccup which was half cry and half laugh escaped her.

Mrs. Blanc's expression softened. "Your father's gone for the doctor. He'll be back soon." She took Lucy gently by the elbow. "Come here and help me."

She had Lucy boil water while she ripped a clean sheet into squares. Lucy knew they were for making compresses to stop bleeding. Her heart sank, but she knew they couldn't have a better nurse for her mother. She ripped some thinner strips for binding William's wound.

Mrs. Blanc took the bloody pad from William's shoulder. She cut his shirt away and they all sat for a moment, regarding the ugly wound. The bullet had plowed through his sleeve, along his upper arm and then back out the coat. He'd bled a lot, and the wound was still oozing.

Mrs. Blanc held up the coat so they could see the hole. "Good news that the bullet passed out, and didn't lodge. But," she frowned at all of them, "It's still a wound. And I want to know how you got yourselves in a position to be taking gunfire."

They looked at each other. Quill nodded toward Lucy and she

gave a brief description of what was happening in Port Townsend, saying simply that they had wound up in the wrong place at the wrong time and that William had taken a stray bullet. She did not say anything about Henry's part in the evening's events.

Mrs. Blanc nodded to herself, as though she'd heard exactly what she expected. She turned the arm toward the light and poured a flask of alcohol over the ragged opening. Will sucked in his breath and tears filled his eyes. "You're going to need that cleaned and stitched by a doctor, not just a part-time trapper's nurse." She re-wrapped the arm and tied it up in a makeshift sling. William was an awful chalky color by the time she was done. He closed his eyes.

"I must say." Mrs. Blanc rubbed her forehead. "You chose quite a night to be out!" She looked sideways at Lucy, who froze, wondering if her lie had been found out.

Lucy wished she'd say something about her mother. Bad news would be better than none. Quill seemed to be feeling the same way. She'd worn a hole in her skirt by picking at it with her fingers, and alternately stared at William's face and out into the night.

"Stay here," said Mrs. Blanc, and Lucy had a strange urge to laugh. Of course they'd stay put! None of them were in much condition to venture out. Where could they go? When Mrs. Blanc left the room, taking some clean linen with her, Lucy went to examine the sink. The cloths were heavily bloodstained, and they weren't all from William.

Quill frowned. "Not her time yet. She's early."

"I know," snapped Lucy.

Shots rang out again, on the uptown side of the woods.

A moment later they heard boots on the porch, the door burst open, and Lucy's father hurried into the room. When he saw her, he took on such a look of white-lipped fury that she leaned into Quill. He shook his head and carried on down the hall, closing the bedroom door with a gentle click.

Everyone settled again. Quill pressed her face against the front window, William leaned his head back against the settee, and Lucy sat at the edge of her seat, barely breathing. A quiet knock broke the silence. "Who's there?" Quill called, laying her hand on the doorknob.

The voice was unintelligible to Lucy, but Quill's face flooded with relief. She wrenched the door open and Henry stumbled into the room.

Relief surged through Lucy. She jumped up and had to resist the urge to touch him. Both girls looked him over. He had a bloody nose and a fat lip, but looked otherwise unharmed. A smile tugged at the corner of his mouth, until Quill pulled her arm back and slapped him so hard his head rocked sideways.

"Really!" Mrs. Blanc exclaimed from the hallway and ordered them all to sit down.

Henry rubbed his jaw. Then he perched, rustling like a bird about to take flight. William opened one eye and gave a wan smile, then closed it again. When the bedroom door opened, a mewling sound escaped. Lucy's father studied her from the hallway. Tears slipped down her cheeks. "Papa, I didn't think."

Her father closed the door gently. He strode down the hall and stopped to stare at her. "You never do. Lucy, you're not five any more!" Lucy's face flamed. Her father ran his fingers through his hair. From the look of him, he'd done that many times in the past few hours.

"Sir," said Henry, rising from his seat. "Altman is headed this way, and he's armed."

Her father looked at him for a moment, then said, "Douse the lights!"

After they'd gotten the house locked up tight, they sat around William in the living room. Lucy's father caught them up on all the night's happenings, parting the curtains every few minutes to look out. "The excitement started this afternoon," he said, "when Katherine Altman went about town, claiming Henry had attacked her." They all protested and he held up a hand. "Hold on! *We* all know that's not the truth, but she told her tale all along Water Street, even pulled her father out of a bar. He shook the girl like a rag doll and said, 'We'll finish them, once and for all.' We know what he was planning, now. But I wonder who the 'we' is?"

Even in the dark, everyone knew he was looking at Henry.

Henry's voice was hard to hear. "Today, I told Altman I was done for good." He sighed. "I tried to quit once, and he said he'd turn me in. But anything is better than working for that man. I won't run his whiskey, and I won't set fires—ever!"

Lucy's father said, "You were seen with Altman downtown, then?"

"I don't know," said Henry, sounding miserable.

"Trust me, you were," her father said, "With all that happened after that, you are in some trouble."

Some? That's an understatement! thought Lucy, and winced when her father said, "Lucy!"

Henry laughed, and Lucy thought. *I have got to get my mouth and my mind uncrossed!*

Her father continued, "Then that millworker showed up, ruffling the town's feathers over how 'a young Indian attacked him.' It fed right into everyone's fears." He held up his hand before Henry could interrupt. "About eight o'clock tonight, someone rang the fire bell—smoke down at Kah Tai. I told the men in town to start up the brigade with the buckets and such."

He took a breath and continued. "Some of them laughed at me, told me, 'No one is going to miss that set of shacks.' They called the fire 'a cleansing.'"

Henry and Quill both hissed.

"I know," her father said. "And I'm sorry." He sighed. "They wouldn't even go wet down Altman's house, close by the village. Judge Swan was nowhere to be seen, so he couldn't help me talk sense into them." He sighed. "A few of us ran around the outside of the village, calling to see if anyone was in there. It took hold so quickly, but thankfully no one seemed to be at home."

"We were at the potlatch," said Quill in a dull voice.

Lucy felt proud that her father had tried to help. She shuddered. What if someone had been inside a house, and her father had gone in to rescue them? What if one of the old Aunties had been in there?

He hesitated again and Lucy's heart sank. "What then?" she asked.

"While we were talking with Mrs. Blanc, your mother arrived, looking for you. And her pains started—all the excitement and rushing up and down the steps," he said, trailing off.

My fault, thought Lucy, with tears welling up.

"We saw soldiers, at North Beach," said William. "Why?"

"Maybe they were called in for the fire," said her father. "But in any event, I think Altman set them after you." He turned toward Henry. "I wouldn't put it past him to lay that fire at your door as well."

"But that's stupid! Why would Henry burn his own village?" William asked.

"Nights like this people shoot first and ask questions after, and Henry's been seen with Altman." He stood up abruptly. "I've got to find that doctor now."

"We can look after things here, sir," said William, sounding so weak, Lucy was sure he'd fall over if he tried to stand up.

"I'll go for the doc!" said Henry, just as booted feet clanked up the front steps and a loud knock sounded on the front door.

"Hide!" whispered her father.

They scrambled into the stairwell. Henry sat halfway up, above Lucy. Quill was one step below her, and William only made it up a few before her father shut the door. When he lit a lamp, the light shone through a crack and Lucy caught a glimpse of William leaning back against Quill's legs for support, her arms curved around him protectively.

That can't be Altman, thought Lucy. The steps were too crisp, too light. Altman always brought with him a feeling of heaviness, in the way he stomped through the world.

The knock came again, louder.

CHAPTER 28

Enemy or Friend?

James," said a deep voice.

"Captain," said her father. Someone struck a match. If Lucy knew her father, he was lighting his pipe, moving very slowly and sending out a feeling of calm. She smiled when she smelled pipe smoke. Lucy felt grateful for his self-control, and wondered now if there'd been other times when he seemed so restful and was actually smoothing over a calamity.

"We're hunting some fugitives. We think they might have come this way."

"I heard the shots," said her father. "Did you figure out who set the fire?"

"*Set* the fire?" The captain sounded surprised. "Well, we're assuming the fire was... well, an accident. But several men took advantage of the situation to loot the other end of town. They got into Cady's pub and the gun shop. So, they're drunk *and* armed."

"That's an unlucky combination," said Lucy's father.

"Indeed."

"How can I help you? We have a baby trying to arrive, and it's not going well."

"Forgive the intrusion," said the captain. "I'm after the doctor. I thought he was here."

"I wish he were!" said Lucy's father. "I'm going back out soon, to look for him."

"I wouldn't if I were you. Not safe by a long shot."

"No choice," said Lucy's father. "What do you need him for?"

"A death certificate."

Everyone shivered.

"Did one of your soldiers get shot?"

"No, sir. An Indian... the one that robbed the pharmacist. One of my men shot him at the pier. He's still down there."

And Altman?

Lucy didn't realize she'd made a sound until Henry's hand gently covered her mouth.

"What was that?" the captain asked, coming toward the door. Lucy held her breath.

Her father cleared his throat loudly. "I hope the man's decently covered?" he asked, "because you'll have to wait. Doc's coming here first." The footsteps moved away, then back. "Touch and go, Captain. Not the first time she's had trouble delivering."

"Oh, I'm sorry, James." A silence followed. Lucy imagined the captain might be putting a hand on her father's shoulder in sympathy. She hadn't met him before but he sounded kind, like Ruby's father.

Henry slid down a step and dropped his hand on hers. She was glad for the dark as a flush raced up her arm to her face. She'd never have imagined this for her first time holding hands! They laced their fingers together, and Lucy found herself thinking of Matthias with a stab of guilt. Much as she liked him, he had nothing like the same effect on her. She felt aflame all along the side that was pressed up against Henry.

"I'll do my best to give you some peace, sir," said the captain as his footsteps drew near once more. "However—"

The stairwell was silent. Not even a breath.

"Is there anything else?" her father asked.

"Well, this is a mite awkward. My men found a canoe beached at the point. Footprints leading right up the beach toward—" He cleared his throat, "—Toward here."

"Did you?" her father asked.

"Ever seen that young Indian boy—used to go about with Altman?" the captain asked. The hand in Lucy's clenched.

"You know I have," said her father, quite loudly. She thought he might be leaning on the stairwell door as pipe smoke seeped in through the cracks. "He studies with me."

"We saw a young Indian at the docks, fighting with Altman, but couldn't tell exactly who it was. I'm assuming it was that boy, and there was a gunshot between them. One of them wounded, my men think."

The voices moved toward the sink and everyone breathed a sigh of relief. "You'll not be touching the cloths for my wife!" said her father.

"That's a lot of cloths for one woman," the captain said. He moved into the front room, with a gritty, grinding sound. Lucy realized they'd dropped sand from their shoes and the captain was scuffing his boots in it. "A lot of sand here," he said.

"What the cloths show you," said her father, interrupting, "is that we need a doctor's help, urgently."

Would the man never leave? She formed the thought ever so quietly in her mind. Henry's other hand moved to cover her lips, as though he knew the thought was about to slip out. If she spoke now, the words against his hand would be like a kiss.

"Don't touch that door!" her father barked by her mother's room. A closet door opened and closed and Lucy almost giggled. Nothing but ladies' underthings in there, nicely washed and pressed by her and Quill. "They say the boy attacked Katherine here, yesterday."

Henry's hand squished Lucy's finger bones together and she let out a little squeak.

"That's not what my daughter says," her father said loudly.

"You found her?" The boots approached again, as though the man were going in tight circles, all of which ended at the stairwell. Lucy thought she might faint from holding her breath. "Yes, thank you Captain. She's upstairs asleep now." A steely edge crept into her father's voice. "Now, if you don't mind?"

One of the soldiers called to the captain from outside. The door opened, there was a murmured conversation and then a gusty sigh. The front door closed again.

"Oh, no! I'm very sorry to hear that," said her father.

"He was a good man, with a family," said the captain.

"Do you know who shot him?"

"No," said the captain. "But most likely one of the two loose in the woods: Altman or that young Clallam."

"I can't imagine that boy killing anyone."

"Altman wouldn't kill a soldier, since he was one."

"Don't let your military bonds blind you! Altman was a deserter." Lucy thought her father must have learned that fact from the Judge.

The captain grunted. "Indeed," he said, but still didn't take his leave.

A woman in labor managed to accomplish what Lucy's father failed to do with all his hints. When her mother cried out in pain, the captain said, "I'll be off! I've got my soldiers heading around the bluff to cut off any escape. They've got the third thief, so the young Indian and Altman are left. We'll have the whole point ringed soon, like a noose."

He spoke once more before leaving. "Keep your doors locked tight and my very best wishes for your wife and baby."

"Thank you, Captain," said Lucy's father. "Best to you and all your men this night. I pray no one else gets hurt."

The captain and his men clattered down the steps. The children waited, listening to Mrs. Blanc's quiet murmurs to her mother from the bedroom.

Lucy was torn between gladness and deep concern when her father insisted on leaving the house. Gladness because he pressed a kiss into her forehead and said, "Your mother will be all right." Concern as she watched him lift his shotgun and walk into the night alone.

Mrs. Blanc relit a few of the lamps so she could see to work. Without thinking, Lucy took one and stood on the porch, watching her father disappear into the trees. She tried to convince herself that he could thread the forest, find the doctor, and do it all safely and in time. One way or another, the baby would be here soon.

Henry stepped out onto the porch. "Mrs. Blanc says to get inside," he said. But he rested an arm across her shoulders and stood with her.

The air was fresh, and the night strangely quiet. For the moment, only frogs and crickets were calling, with the occasional *who, who* of an owl. They both jumped when large wings flapped in front of them, and the owl glided by. Lucy shivered, sure a soul had departed on the wings of that ghostly-gray bird.

She had no desire to go inside and listen to her mother's suffering, if she couldn't do anything to help. She set the lamp down, and it felt like the most natural thing in the world to rest her head on Henry's shoulder, with her arm around his waist. She felt his warmth flow into her.

"I suppose you're the one in the most danger," she said. "Especially after that poor soldier. I keep thinking of him lying there on the steps, dead."

Henry sat down hard on the front step. "They're so quick to blame us, whenever a soldier's killed." He stared out into the darkness. Lucy was about to sit down next to him when a figure lurched out of the darkness, hesitated, and then turned toward them. Lucy froze.

"See you're workin' on the teacher's daughter now, *partner*. Like you did with mine."

Henry's body tensed, but he said, "Why are you here, Altman?" in a different voice than he'd used before, a stronger voice. He stood up.

"Why?" Altman's laugh ended in a dry rattle. "You need my help! Come down here, now," Altman said. "Help me paddle that canoe you left." Altman's voice turned Lucy's insides to jelly and Henry leaned forward, as though to obey.

"He didn't hurt Katherine," said Lucy, stepping in front of Henry. The awful man seemed to have a strange power over him. "He stopped her from hurting me."

"Yeahhh, sure he did," said Altman, making those few words sound so dirty.

Henry lunged toward Altman, and it took all Lucy's strength to hold him back. "Don't," she hissed. "Don't let him rile you into something stupid! He wants you down there so he can grab you!" Lucy held onto Henry and peered out into the darkness, hoping for help.

"I can draw him away from here, from you and Quill and your mother," Henry whispered. Lucy tried to think. Surely the soldiers would be coming this way soon? Maybe she could string out the conversation. She'd heard Altman could be a fountain of speech when telling stories in the saloon. Her mind boiled, yet nothing came out. When she most needed the words, they stayed locked inside. Henry didn't seem to have anything to say, either.

"Don't!" she said, priming the pump on her flow of words. "Don't do anything you'll regret!"

Altman laughed. "That the best you got?" he called. Lucy realized he was playing with them. "What do you care, book girl?" he added.

She stiffened. Was he referring to the book Katherine had killed? He continued to chuckle, and Lucy felt a white-hot anger sear through her. "You'll go to jail!" she said.

"For taking care of that coward next to you? Who'll care if I gun the Injun down after he killed a soldier?"

"He didn't!" she said.

"They're lookin' for him already!" Altman staggered a little and Lucy feared he'd shoot them by accident. "If I shoot him, they'll call it justice. That soldier? He got in my way on the stairs to uptown, just like you are now. He's lying in a pool of his own blood."

For the second time that night, Lucy saw Altman come toward her, pointing a gun at her chest. She didn't think he would risk shooting a girl, but her whole body went cold. She wedged herself against Henry, who muttered, "Lucy, stop it! I'll not let you be in the middle of this."

"I'll shoot right through the pair of you, if you don't get out of the way." Altman dropped his staggering and drunken slurs, and spoke with a dead-level tone. Lucy realized some of his stumbling was an act, and that he might be much smarter than she'd realized. Fear choked her, but scuffling with Henry broke its grip and she could think again. Her eyes fell on the lantern. At the same time, she heard the blessed sound of someone crashing through the trees.

"Get out of the way!" bellowed Altman just as Henry said, "Lucy, MOVE!" and grabbed her shoulders. Lucy lashed out and kicked the lantern.

The lamp shattered and went out. A shot rang out, and there was a moment of silence.

Darkness cloaked the scene.

The front door burst open and Quill flew out. Shouts from the far side of the clearing told Lucy the soldiers had arrived. Torches appeared in the trees. Lucy sought Henry's figure on the porch, and she wilted with relief. He pointed to the splintered beam above his head, where a bullet had lodged in the wood.

Altman was nowhere to be seen.

"Get inside Henry, quick, and don't argue!" Lucy said.

She and Quill told the soldiers the perfect lie: that William, in the front room looking pale, had been the one on the porch. She had to admire Quill's quickness. She cut the bandages off and pressed them against the wound, as though he'd just been shot. William played the part by groaning loudly, and had a real wound to show by way of proof.

"Bastard shot me," William said, through gritted teeth.

The captain said, "If you weren't Brinnon's son," and stared hard at William for a moment. But Will rested his head back, looking like he was about to faint. The captain left after a moment, reminding them once again to keep inside with everything locked up tight.

After that everything moved so quickly. Her father returned with a harassed looking doctor in tow. Mrs. Blanc convinced her father to take Lucy and the others to her house. Lucy knew her mother was in danger and they wanted everyone out of the way.

The sounds of the chase disappeared over the hill toward the beach and they were left alone at the house. Her father gave quick orders. William, Henry and Quill left with Lucy and her father. As they entered the woods, a poke from behind made Lucy yelp. Henry pulled her into the trees and whispered, "Someone's out there." She could feel his breath on her hair.

They'd stepped behind the familiar cedar tree. Quill and William joined them, with William leaning into the tree's bulk. Lucy's father stood his ground on the path.

In the deep silence of the woods, a twig snapped.

"Who's there?" her father called out. "Show yourself!"

"Is that you, James?" someone called, and Lucy wanted to scream. The last thing they needed was to wait again, forever, while her father had a long conversation. They needed to get William somewhere safe to rest, and Henry out of sight. She felt an odd sense, as if they might never make it to a safe rest, never end their wanderings. The night had been so long.

"Sheriff," said her father, "Why are you out here?"

The sheriff's lamp cast a ghostly light into the branches above their heads. "I might ask you that same question, my friend."

Her father explained about the baby.

"It's a savage night to be about!" the sheriff said. "Two dead so far, and I'm on the lookout for a young Clallam. He'll have a sore accounting when we find him."

"What makes you so sure this young man's done wrong?" her father asked.

"Trust me, I know. He's one and parcel with the others they're hunting out there."

"And you're out looking as well?"

"Actually, no," The sheriff said slowly. "Katherine Altman's up at my house, with her hands terribly burned. She came to our house with all her brothers and sisters trailing behind her like ducks. Some had hair burned off, and the littlest will be lucky not to get an infection on her arm where the skin's gone."

"How awful!" said Lucy's father. "They're all my students. What happened to them?"

"Katherine got them out of the house before it burned down. She scorched her hands wrenching the window open." His voice stuck on the next words. "It's an ugly thing. That Altman, he locked them in and left. Then, with the flames raging in the Indian village next door."

Lucy felt sick at what Altman had done. She didn't think anyone could burn his own children. Perhaps he was trying to protect them by keeping them out of the way? But surely he'd realized that he was setting a fire right next door?

"I'll send the doctor, after," said her father, "but Amelia's having a difficult time; the girl will have to wait."

"Katherine's in terrible pain. Keeps mumbling about her father coming back."

"I expect the man will be dead by morning," said her father. "Killed a soldier."

"Did he now? I thought it was the young Clallam that did it."

Her father grunted. In his weariness, he'd left the door open for the sheriff's sharp mind. "I'm sure that can't be right," he said stubbornly.

After a moment the sheriff said, "I won't keep you any longer."

Lucy peeked around the tree. The two men were shaking hands.

"Tell the doctor about Katherine, please. And James, best wishes for a safe delivery."

"Thank you," said her father, gesturing for the sheriff to go ahead of him. "You might as well go home," he said. "I'll keep an eye out for the doc, and send him your way when we can." They moved off toward town together. After a long wait, Lucy and her friends followed them.

CHAPTER 29

Waiting and Hoping

Quill's hands were tucked under her face. She was sound asleep in Mrs. Blanc's giant four poster bed, next to Lucy. The moon had risen high, and Lucy was sure its light draped everything below in an eerie beauty. Not for the first time, she wondered how the weather could be so out of step with human happenings. It could be so beautiful when something sad was going on, and so gloomy at times of joy and celebration.

The crash of the waves echoed up to her, strong against the headland they'd paddled around not so many hours before. Lucy thought of the boy upstairs—the feel of his breath on her hair, and his arm along her shoulders. She thought of all the possibilities that might stretch ahead of her, if things were different. Tomorrow, she'd have to let go of them all; if she didn't she would lose him to prison, or worse.

No one had seen Altman kill the soldier. No one could prove it hadn't been Henry. Except herself, with her word about what Altman had confessed. But who would believe a girl who'd run away from her family, or an Indian who'd broken the law?

Worries about Henry gave way to thoughts of her mother. Lucy knew Mrs. Blanc and the doctor were caring for her, but she wished she could be there. It was terrible imagining what might be happening.

As soon as they'd reached Mrs. Blanc's, her father had said, "I'll be back in the morning."

She'd nodded. "What if?" she'd started. "What if Mama—?" She needed to tell her mother how sorry she was for running away, and for causing pain and worry and possibly bringing the birth on early. *What if Mama dies and I never see her again?*

Suddenly, the birds were calling, and bustling sounds floated up from the waterfront. Lucy crept out of bed and looked through the window. The ships were returning to pick up their moorings in the harbor, now that the fire had burnt itself out. She left Quill asleep, twisted up in the blankets as though she'd been fighting something.

Lucy fetched a pitcher and went down to Mrs. Blanc's cellar. She pulled a pot of butter out of the stream that ran under the house. The place held a cool mist like a mysterious cave. Lucy remembered her delight the first time she'd seen where Mrs. Blanc kept her butter: in a crock in a stream, inside. Lucy went back upstairs. She put the kettle on to boil, and was crumbling some leaves into the teapot when the clip-clop of a horse reminded her of the plan she'd concocted in the middle of the night. She splashed some water over her face and went out, hoping the cart was from Bishop's Dairy.

How was she to be with Matthias now? Would he sense the change in her? But she realized her feelings toward him hadn't actually changed. She'd been more than a little flattered by his attentions. But she knew now that she'd felt only a warm friendship, nothing more. She hoped he wouldn't feel mistreated.

A moment later Matthias turned the corner, with his hat pushed back on his head and a stalk of straw between his teeth. Lucy had to smile at the sight of his amiable face, so steady and comforting after the night she'd had. She smoothed her hair, and the dress she'd spent the night in, then hurried out to stop him before the next delivery.

"Lucy," he said, climbing down and reaching to take her hands. She avoided his clasp, pretending to dry her hands on the apron she'd pulled from a kitchen drawer. "Mornin'," he said, looking puzzled as he left his hands midair for a moment, then dropped them. "How's your mother?"

"I don't know yet," she said, feeling a stab of worry.

They both were quiet. Then Matthias spoke, "I'm sorry for your friends. A few of the farm hands came down last night to watch the village burn." He frowned. "Some say it's a good thing. But I can't think on another's misfortune that way myself... even if we have had some disagreements."

"What's it like close up?"

"Not much left but blackened timbers," he said. "It's a sorrowful sight: people all over the place, crying and digging through the rubble." He sighed. "It's dangerous, with houses collapsing and nails sticking out all over the place. And the smell is horrid. Burnt."

Matthias took everything in stride, like Lucy's father. He hadn't asked her why she was here, at Mrs. Blanc's. He turned to fill a jar with milk from a big steel jug. When he pushed aside the burlap wrappings, she had the finishing touches for her idea.

"Matthias, would you help us?" she asked. "After you finish your deliveries?"

They were drinking hot tea with lemon drops. A sleepy Quill sat at the table with a blanket wrapped around her shoulders. Henry walked into the kitchen. "I'm so sore from paddling!" He rubbed his chest and stretched, and his eyes lit up when he looked at Lucy. His dimple flashed in his cheek, then disappeared as he looked out the window.

Lucy's heart skipped a beat, then settled again. She didn't know what to say.

Footsteps pounded on the porch and they all tensed. Judge Swan came in, looking tired. "I've spoken to the Chief," he said, without any small talk. "There's too much trouble for Henry to stay in town." He turned to the boy. "Chetzmoka can't keep you here, son."

Henry nodded. Lucy moved her chair close to his.

"He said your uncle—the one who came for the potlatch—he can take you to Vancouver Island until things settle down. If we can get you to Discovery Bay, he'll leave today."

"Today?" Lucy asked. "But, it's all so wrong! Can't you do anything?"

"I don't believe Henry's done more than choose his friends badly," said the judge. "And carry some, uh... items for others. But I
wouldn't want to risk a trial. You never know who'll sit on a jury,
and what their opinions might be. There's a—well, a *momentum*
going in this town, and it's not in favor of the tribe."

Henry nodded in agreement, with a dazed look in his eyes.

Before he left, Henry pulled Lucy into the garden at the side of the
house. Lucy knew she would remember forever the complicated
scent of roses blooming on a warm morning, and the salty air of a
tide change, with a bitter hint of ash.

"What will you do there?" she asked. "On Vancouver's Island?"

"Maybe marry a star!" he said. "Remember? It's my uncle who
cut stars in his roof!"

"I like your uncle," said Lucy. She smiled at him, but felt an
ache as she thought about the days that stretched ahead with no
Henry to pop out of a bush, or lean over her on his bow while she
read aloud, or touch her hand. An ache for Quill as well, as she
stayed on without her brother's companionship.

"I did not kill anyone," he said, looking more serious than she'd
ever seen him, "and I did not burn that house in Chimacum. I was
only the lookout. We sold bottles before, but then Altman started
burning and stealing." He shook his head sharply, as though trying to clear it of unwanted images. "I quit."

She nodded. "I believe you." During the night, with Altman
and the guns, she had wondered for a moment. But in the light of
day, the thought of Henry hurting anyone was absurd.

"I *will* do something good," he said, "like your hunchback who
helped the Gypsies." He pressed her hand. "And loved his Gypsy girl," he said, his gaze making her warm. Henry's eyes reminded her of the sea. She loved the deeper feelings that moved under
the surface, though he didn't give them voice. At the moment, she
could read them clearly.

"I know you will," said Lucy, reaching up a finger to touch
his dimple.

"I would like to hear the end of the story someday."

"Someday, you'll read it yourself," she said, trying to keep her voice firm. She didn't tell him that the ending was good, but also very sad. The hunchback might find a way through, but the Gypsy girl would not.

Matthias came back in a hurry. The sheriff's men were asking about Henry, he said, so they needed to move. With a little maneuvering, Henry was soon under the burlap, and Lucy, Quill and the judge were left standing in the road as the milk wagon pulled away. Matthias sat up on the box alone, with a strange expression on his face.

The judge patted her arm. "Brilliant idea, Lucy," he said.

She thought of the jugs they'd pulled out of the wagon and stacked in Mrs. Blanc's basement, to make room for Henry. Hopefully, no one would look too closely at Matthias' cart. Henry would have to stay under the burlap a long while, as the wagon traced the new road from Port Townsend to Discovery Bay. The uncle waited with his canoe ready, and Lucy's heart ached at the thought of Henry getting in and gliding away, like that very first time she'd seen him.

Quill stayed behind to watch over William until the judge could get him a doctor and a ride back to Brinnon. Lucy was sick of waiting and hiding. Women were walking about, gossiping and loitering on the cliff above Quill's Village. The soldiers had all returned to their post, so the town must be safe now.

Lucy patted William, told Quill to come to their house as soon as she could, and set off for home at last. Halfway up the path she heard steps, but rather than jumping behind her tree she set her feet and put her hands on her hips. Her father's face lit up when he saw her, but he was so haggard and pale.

She was afraid to ask. They stood looking at each other for a moment.

"It's a boy!" he said, picking her up and twirling her around. "And your mother should recover fine!" He put her down, ruffling her hair.

A funny twist in his voice made her uneasy. "I'm older now.

Please, tell me."

"She's lost a lot of blood, Lulu," he admitted, "but the doc says she'll make it, especially with you and Mrs. Blanc nursing her." He smiled, a tired smile, and she noticed new wrinkles around his mouth. As they walked, he gave her all the news. The baby was strong, much like she had been. Lucy marveled. Rough as it was, Port Townsend had given them a healthy baby.

The captain had returned at dawn and her father had shown him over the house. He told the man truthfully that Lucy had been sent to Mrs. Blanc's to sleep, somehow forgetting to mention that she'd had company.

"Did they catch Altman?" asked Lucy.

Her father shook his head. "The waves did. His body washed up this morning at Point Wilson. Guess he tried to manage those currents in a small canoe that was left on our beach, by some unknown person or persons." Lucy felt his eyes on her. "It would take a miracle to get around the point in a strong wind, wouldn't it?" he said. "I'd love to hear from anyone who had! Though I'd hate to think of someone I loved being out in such a storm." He scratched his chin. "And I wouldn't mention it to your mother, ever."

His pace picked up as they approached home. "The law would have done worse if they'd caught Altman. Even if they don't believe he killed that soldier, he wounded another while getting away. Added to the break-ins and theft, they would have hanged him quick."

"Does Katherine know?" asked Lucy.

"No, Lucy. The child's too ill, with a fever and her burns."

When they reached the house, a part of Lucy that had been tense all summer relaxed. From the door of the bedroom, she searched her mother's face. She looked pale but normal. Lucy took a deep breath and went forward into the room.

"I'm so glad to have you back," was all her mother said. She patted the bed. "Sit here."

Lucy heard the little squeaks and nuzzles of her brother in the crook of her mother's arm—Justice James, for so he had been named. Her mother lifted the baby so Lucy could greet him. He was wrinkled and red like a tiny gnome, with bright blue eyes.

"A gift!" said her mother, "like you!"

"Not me," said Lucy, choking back tears. "Not lately!" But her mother shushed her and they sat together with the baby. Lucy snuggled the warm bundle, planting a kiss on his soft cheek. The baby fell asleep in her arms, and soon her mother drifted off as well. Lucy didn't like how waxy her mother's skin looked, but her breathing seemed deep and easy.

"I'll keep an eye on her," her father whispered, taking the baby in one arm and pushing her toward the stairs. "Get some rest. We'll need you even more, now!"

Lucy ached for sleep, but a few things needed settling first. "Papa?"

"What is it?" He asked with his old gentleness, and Lucy knew the world had spun round and come back into its proper orbit, almost.

"I need to do some things, later. Do you think I could go downtown?"

He was very still. The baby burped and he laughed. "I do believe," he said, giving her a stern look, "I truly do believe you can manage yourself well, if you will only *think*!"

She nodded.

"Promise to bring yourself back here at a responsible time, so as not to cause your mother, myself, or the whole town any more worry."

"I'm sorry, Father," she said softly. "I promise."

"Get some rest," he said again.

Only then, up in her room at the end of that remarkable night and morning, was she able to think about a moment in the garden at Mrs. Blanc's.

She warmed from the crown of her head to her sandy shoes as she relived the moment: His face, blocking out the dawn sky as he leaned in, smiled, and surprised her by continuing all the way in, laying a gentle and slow pressure on her mouth. He brushed his lips across her cheek, so lightly that it felt like a breeze blowing past. He lifted a thick handful of her hair, and then tipped her chin to stare into her eyes, as though memorizing her. Then he took each of her hands in turn and held kissed them.

With a mischievous half-smile, he'd turned and walked around the house to the wagon that would take him away, looking back once before climbing under the burlap.

The flame that had been kindling in her since he'd taught her the word for limpet on the windswept island had burst into a full-fledged blaze. Musing over her diary, she drew spirals in the margin. She'd felt a thrill when Matthias noticed her, because of his age and the way all the other girls fluttered around him. But he treated her like a younger sister. When Henry spoke to her he came along side, right at her elbow, or crouched down next to her. She wished she could go back to the small island with him today and eat strawberries, run barefoot on the beach, and watch the blue-green waves wash forward and back, ruffled in white foam. But she could not.

She'd said her goodbye. Tomorrow she'd have to say another that was equally hard.

Lucy slept the whole of that morning away.

In the hot hours of the afternoon, she took out Quill's handiwork. It didn't take long to sell the pretty baskets. Mothers and sisters of classmates bought them to put their hair combs in. They thanked Lucy prettily, and the coins clinked in her pocket as she walked.

Mrs. Blanc bought four, pulling more coins than necessary out of her beaded purse and dropping them into Lucy's pocket with a pat. "I'll be up to see all of you later, with a cake!" Then she laid her hand on Lucy's. "We can talk."

Some of the mothers did not look happy to see Lucy on their doorstep, though even the older girls looked at her with a new respect, almost awe. She wondered if it was for running away, kissing a boy, or ordering Katherine Altman off her property. Perhaps for all three! She stood a little taller.

Most people asked about her mother and brother, for which she was grateful. After a few more houses, she'd sold all but one basket.

After finishing *Hunchback,* Lucy had decided that in a way Katherine was more like the lonely soul in the bell tower than Henry and Quill could ever be. They had their uncles, and aunties and the tribe. Lucy had her own family and Mrs. Blanc and the school and Bekah and the Bishops and Judge Swan. But who did Katherine have, especially now?

She wondered if Katherine would wind up in the orphanage she'd spoken of with such fear, up north. Lucy tried not to imagine the drowned man on the beach, there where the tides always turned, casting secrets back into the open. She wondered if Katherine knew, yet, what the waves had washed up this time.

Ruby was out on the lawn of her house, playing hide and seek with Katherine's sisters and brothers. The bandages on legs and arms told Lucy the doctor had paid his visit. Ruby gave her a crooked grin and a wave. Lucy knew her avid curiosity would lead her to pester Lucy later, even though Ruby's father could tell her anything she'd like to know. Someday, Lucy thought, Ruby would become a news reporter—one of those that wrote shocking headlines.

Extra, Extra! Read all about it! Teacher's daughter wreaks havoc.

Small town in Washington Territory will never be the same.

Ruby's mother spoke in a hushed voice at the front door. "Can I help you?"

"Would you give Katherine this?" Lucy held up a basket. She'd chosen the prettiest one and filled it with wildflowers, early blackberries, a goldfinch feather, and a peppermint. She'd added some coins from the pile in her pocket, feeling she could spare that much from her goal.

Ruby's mother looked surprised. "Come in. You can give it to her yourself."

"Sure," mumbled Lucy, following her up the stairs. *Get a handle on yourself!* she told herself, as Altman's face swam into her mind.

Looking back over her shoulder, Ruby's mother said, "Did you say something, dear?"

"No, Ma'am."

Pushing Lucy into the room, Ruby's mother whispered, "Keep it brief. She's got a fever."

The girl on the bed was asleep, her face flushed and her hair wet with sweat. Her hands lay on top of the quilt, shrouded in bandages. Her eyes opened and turned toward Lucy, who was struck by the pain she saw there, and by how young and clean Katherine's face was above the white coverlet.

"Where's Papa?" Katherine asked.

No one had told her, then. Lucy pulled up a chair and sat close, with the basket on her lap. One thing she knew of Katherine, she'd want the truth. Best prepare her gently.

"He's left, Katherine," said Lucy, "Left in a canoe last night."

The girl's hands jerked, then she sucked in air with a pained sound. Lucy didn't know if the fear in her eyes was *of* her father, or *for* her father, or—

"Carl? Lacy? Mariah?"

Lucy put her hand on the girl's hair, as her mother would do. When Katherine glared, Lucy took it away. "They're all fine! Outside, playing with Ruby." Lucy smiled, then pulled the window open. "Can't you hear them?" Dog barks and children's squeals floated up to them.

Katherine relaxed a little. "They like dogs," she said, with something close to a smile. "We used to have one a'fore Papa killed it." The smile evaporated and she quit talking.

Not knowing what to say, Lucy held the basket out. "I've brought you some things, and a basket to put them into."

"What things? Ain't got no things now."

"Well, I've put some in for you. Just a few, but it's a beginning." Lucy took out the feathers and flowers one by one, laying them across the blanket. The golden rose she'd picked at Mrs. Blanc's made a sunny splash on the crocheted quilt.

"Why?" demanded the girl.

"I don't know," said Lucy, getting frustrated. Then she thought of Quill patiently teaching her to weave. "Sometimes," Quill had told her, "you throw many pieces on the floor before you find the right strip for a basket. Try again. Try something new."

Lucy tried again. "I guess the things that happened at the quilting bee were as much my fault as yours. I'm sorry for what I said." It was all true, but Lucy knew she shouldn't have said it. She felt a shift in the atmosphere of the room, an easing; but the fever was harassing the girl again. Katherine turned her head toward the wall.

"I'll be going." Lucy put the basket on the table. "Bye, Katie."

"It's Katherine to you!"

Lucy heard something of the girl's spirit returning, and her own stubbornness rose up.

"Well, goodbye then!" she said, and hurried from the room. But once she was out, something turned her around, like a hand tapping her on the shoulder. She tiptoed back to the open door. Katherine was awkwardly lifting the pieces with her wrapped hands, examining each one in turn and then placing them back, tenderly, in the basket.

Lucy's heart softened toward the girl, and she left feeling glad she'd made the effort. She hurried downstairs, said goodbye to Ruby, and picked up her pace on the way home. She felt the need to check on her mother, to reassure herself that she and the baby were still well.

One meeting over, she thought, *the hardest yet to come.*

Early in the morning, Quill came up over the path from the meadow with something bulky in her arms. She staggered toward Lucy, who sat on the front steps next to a stack of neatly wrapped packages.

"We're leaving now," said Quill, "for Jamestown, past Sequim.

We have an uncle there, who has bought us a piece of land."

"I know," said Lucy, swallowing the lump in her throat. "Judge Swan told me."

Quill set down the large basket. "I have brought gifts from me, from my aunties," she looked at Lucy with a smile, "and from Henry."

A thrill ran through Lucy, but she waited for Quill to speak.

Gazing at the house, the steps, and the clearing, Quill said, "I will miss these. This is one of my places, now."

Lucy had promised herself not to make things worse for Quill, so she didn't say what she was thinking: that the place could never be quite right without the twins around. She chose the first package on the stack and held it out to her friend. "I hope you like them."

Quill unwrapped the gloves and held them up to her cheek. "Like a princess wears?"

Nodding, Lucy said, "You are a princess, so they will be. Do you want to put them on?"

"I will save them," said Quill, tucking them into her pocket. From the look on her face, Lucy knew she'd chosen well. Quill nodded toward the basket, and Lucy looked more closely. It was big, like the one Katherine had broken, but this one had a yellow sun worked into the reeds.

"From my brother," she said. "He wanted you to have it."

Lucy lifted the lid. Down in the bottom was a trembling bit of fluff. She scooped up two big ears and a tiny body. "Poor thing," Lucy said, holding the baby rabbit close and making soothing noises, as Quill stroked its sides.

"He found it right before he left with our uncle. Will you have him?"

"Of course!" The name for the rabbit was obvious. "I'll call him Henry, and hope he doesn't get into nearly as much trouble!"

Lucy handed Quill the big package, and several small ones. Quill lit up when she opened the slate. Lucy had put chalk into a red pencil box her grandmother had sent out from Boston. She'd wrapped up a small primer, and 'borrowed' one of the *Advanced*

Readings from the school. She'd also bought a journal with a red cover, a silver quill pen and ink. Lucy had sketched a small quail on the inside cover, and written:

Q is for Quail, and Quill! Best of luck, love, Egg-Among-the-Shells.

Quill smiled at the pen and the drawing, and ran her hands over the creamy-white pages of the journal, then over each other item. Her face clouded. "This all cost too much!"

"No," said Lucy firmly, "it didn't. Some of it was mine to give, and we have school stuff! But you earned the rest with your quick fingers. Truly."

"The baskets?" Quill asked. Lucy nodded and Quill's face cleared. "Lucy, you must practice weaving. Nothing comes in a moment," she added sadly, "even if it can go so quickly."

Each had one last gift. Lucy put an English story she'd gotten from Mrs. Blanc into her friend's hands, saying, "For Henry." She wrinkled her brow, finding words. "Tell him, read this. I know he can do it." She looked at Quill, then said, "Ask him to write to me a line or two? I know he's not one to say much. Maybe a sketch?"

"Lucy," Quill began, her voice a warning.

"What?"

"That never works."

"What doesn't?" Lucy played dumb, not ready to talk about the lingering blush of feeling along her lips where Henry had kissed her.

Quill continued on as though Lucy hadn't spoken. "A friend of my mother's married her love—a white man—and moved into his house. One of those big ones with a porch, near Sequim. She must have been in love because she was the most beautiful girl, and a princess too." Quill shook her head. "She could have married anyone she wanted, like a chief."

From Quill's tone, Lucy knew this wasn't going to end well. "Please," she hooked her arm through Quill's. "It's such a beautiful morning!"

Quill looked sideways, not quite turning her head enough to look Lucy in the eye. "She hung herself." Lucy dropped her arm and Quill continued, "No one knows what was said, but they found out later that her husband's sister payed a visit unexpectedly—from the east coast! She didn't know her brother had married an Indian girl, and assumed the woman who answered the door was a servant. The beautiful wife was there alone, keeping her house and making pies. When the husband and sons came back, the wife was dead and the sister nowhere to be seen."

"Why would she do that?" Lucy whispered.

"The S'Klallam girl, or the horrible sister?"

"Both! The S'Klallam girl, I guess. Why not tell the horrible sister to go away?"

"They think the wife couldn't live with the insult and shame. Her way to protest."

"I figured it was something like that," Lucy said. "But I'm only fourteen, and he's gone." The face that reminded her so much of Henry's, the second half of the apple, nodded and she felt that stab of separation again, doubly. She would have neither half now.

So many disappointments. Lucy recalled the look on Matthias' face as he flicked the burlap over Henry in the back of his wagon. She thought he'd missed the kiss, but she saw hurt there, and disappointment—all the things she knew she'd find in her father's face if he were to find out about that morning. But her father would not find out. Matthias was angry, but he wasn't the type to tattle. *Ruby, on the other hand....* Lucy shuddered at the thought of what Ruby could do with such a tasty tidbit, but Ruby needn't know about Lucy and Henry.

They found Lucy's mother in a chair, with the baby wrapped in his sea-colored quilt. Quill laid a bundle on her lap and she unwrapped it. Inside were two tiny moccasins, decorated with blue beads. Lucy's mother exclaimed over the precise handiwork, delighted.

"We made them together," said Quill, "the aunties and I, from skins my father brought. The good wish is from him as well." Quill took the baby in her arms, kissed his sleeping cheek and brushed his fat little feet with her hands.

"I'm so sorry, Quill, for your village." Lucy's mother held up the moccasins, "I don't know how you found the time or peace to make these. Thank you." Lucy noticed the shells on the laces, which jingled softly. Following her gaze, Quill said, "Those are to help you find him. When he wanders away like Lucy!"

Lucy's mother laughed, and she let Lucy go to the meadow with Quill. As they came down toward the water, a shadow fell over Lucy's heart. In the bay floated the canoes, twenty or so, with all Quill's people waiting. Ash smudged many faces, and the aunties looked numb and slack-jawed, lacking the bustling energy Lucy had always sensed beneath their surface.

"We have been searching for days, but there is little left," said Quill, and her voice dropped to a whisper. "Hope is a hard thing to give up."

The meadow looked as green as when they'd first met, on this same path. The butterflies, flowers and sun were all present. Lucy wondered how days could look so alike, but feel so different. She said, "Maybe you will find something whole out of the shells, like my eggs."

"I hope so," Quill said. "I will come back to visit, in time to gather salmonberries."

Lucy nodded, her spirits sinking lower. That was almost a year away.

They embraced, and her friend waded out to the nearest canoe. A different young man waited with his paddle, holding the boat. Lucy didn't even try to push down the tears that welled up inside her. One of the aunties lifted her hand in a half-hearted wave, and Quill turned back and waved as well. The tears spilled over and ran down Lucy's face.

Suddenly she caught the scent, like her first day in this meadow by the water. Lucy wondered if she'd ever find it again—that mix of sea and cedar, salt and a tang of mystery that swirled around Quill and Henry that first morning. Would Port Townsend feel complete without that particular combination? Without the S'Klallam half of the town?

Today, an undertone of smoke hit her. Not the pleasant al-
der smoke of salmon-curing fires in the summer under a canopy
of stars, but the acrid aftertaste of the fire that had taken everything from Quill's family. Lucy realized that the fire had robbed
her too, as the scent left her, bobbing along the waves with the de-
parting canoes. She would miss the canoe rides and the gathering,
the weaving and the working together at chores and words, the
berries and the way Henry in particular had taught her to see and
taste everything.

Slowly, like a funeral train, the line of canoes moved into the
current, pushing out into choppy water. They turned west, toward
Clallam Bay and all the little bays that lay between. Lucy stood
alone, watching until they slipped into the bank of fog that so often cloaked this stretch of water, and disappeared from sight.

CHAPTER 30

B is for Beginning, Again

Lucy missed Quill and Henry sorely. When she wasn't holding Justice James or scrubbing laundry, she wandered the woods and beaches near home. A few days before the New Year, she stopped by her old boot on the beach. The day was cold but clear, and the boot had flipped over and was filled with water, reflecting the sky. When she peered inside, she found a miniature tide pool, with a tiny starfish, some baby anemones, and one small tunsu'etc, clinging to the side. The boot seemed to have changed its message.

Winter brought extra time, and she collected items for the Smithsonian or brought things back to sketch in her room, with the little rabbit at her feet. Her eyes often drifted to the window and the sky beyond. She sketched Quill as she remembered her, looking toward Point Wilson with her hair blowing behind her; and Henry with his bow and part of his face in shadow. She wished he were here to laugh at her when something inappropriate escaped from her mouth, and she missed the warmth of sitting squished into the canoe with Quill.

One of her drawings was of Katherine's hands, which had healed up tight and curled. She and Lucy had forged an uneasy truce: Katherine submitted to Lucy's help with lessons because she couldn't hold chalk or pencil, and Lucy learned to ignore the girl's comments. Lucy often felt Matthias' eyes on her at those moments. She hoped they'd be friends again soon, but his hurt look had gradually turned to resentment, and Lucy wasn't sure if she could ever recover his good opinion. The girls back in Boston agreed that she should try to retrieve the first boy, now the second one had left. But Lucy couldn't think that way. Matthias wasn't a dress or shoes to be picked up and dropped on a whim.

One particularly blustery February day, while the children huddled over their lessons and the stove sputtered in the corner, a dapper Indian in a bowler hat opened the door and ushered in a young lady.

"Quill!" cried Lucy, jumping up.

"Chetzmoka!" said her father, going forward, "Welcome!" He held out both his hands to clasp the chief's.

The chief took them and said, "My niece has come to live with Jenny Lind and me. I have spoken with her father, and we would like for her to attend your school."

All eyes went to Quill, who was dressed neatly in clothes Mrs. Blanc had given her before she left. Her thick braid was pinned up in a neat coil, and she wore a dark red dress. Lucy thought she looked more like a woman now than a girl, and felt a little shy with her.

A frown furrowed Katherine's forehead, and other faces showed everything from anger to curiosity. Ruby was grinning from ear to ear. A buzz of whispers started in the back of the room and moved forward.

"Like she can talk!" a younger version of Katherine piped up, followed by snickers.

"Children!" said her father in a sharp voice, as Quill moved toward a seat at the back of the class. Chetzmoka's expression was difficult to read.

Not this time! thought Lucy, feeling Quill's gaze.

She took a deep breath and stood up, curtseyed to Quill's uncle and turned to face the class. "I'd like to introduce my friend, Quill," Lucy said. "She is Chief Chetzmoka's niece, and can help anyone who's struggling with reading." From the corner of her eye, she saw the chief's nod and the look of approval he gave her.

Quill smiled at the class and said, "I'm very happy to meet you."

Then Lucy took Quill's arm and led her to the place she'd always belonged: in the seat next to hers, at the front of the class.

HISTORY: BEHIND THE STORY

Earliest known photo of Port Townsend: Water Street, ca. 1862
University of Washington (UW) Libraries, Special Collections, UW23139z

Places

Alfred Plummer Cabin: In April of 1851, Alfred Plummer and Charles Bachelder staked the first official claim in Port Townsend and built their cabin by the beach, then sent for their families. In the early years, most goods were traded or bartered. Fresh water had to be hauled in, making everyday chores difficult.

First cabin in Port Townsend, built in 1851
by Alfred Plummer
UW Libraries, Special Collections, UW5082

Castle House at Fort Worden (Lucy's House): I placed Lucy's house at present day Fort Worden, a state park and former military base; also a favorite place for our family. Castle House was built at that location by the Reverend John Alexander in 1883. Sadly, when he went home to fetch his Scottish sweetheart, she'd already married another so he never lived there. Lucy's house would have been built of wood, as no stone or brick was used until the 1880s.

Ebey House and Ferry House: Ebey Reserve now holds hiking paths, a beach and active farms. It includes Isaac's parents' house and the Ferry House. After Isaac's death, his wife had their cabins pulled apart and the boards used to build a guest house, still called *The Ferry House*. The ferry landed there until it was moved to its current location. Ferries have always been important to life on the Peninsula, and every adventure began with a ferry ride when I was small.

Author visits Ferry House

Ad for the "new" Ferry House at Ebey's Landing
Port Townsend Register, January 18, 1860; UW Libraries, Special Collections, 1860018.002

Kahtai: qatáy

S'Klallam Settlement at Kahtai: Kah Tai is the original name for Port Townsend. Some place the S'Klallam houses at Point Hudson, but Swan notes that the 'Chemakum' lived at Point Hudson and the S'Klallam by the lagoon on the other side of town. I've placed them at Swan's location, on the way to Chimacum.

222

Little Boston, Port Gamble: nəxʷqʼíyt

Port Gamble: This mill town halfway between the Kingston Ferry and Port Townsend looks much as it did in the mid 1800s. A S'Klallam village there agreed to move when the mill was built, and the Port Gamble S'Klallam still live across the small inlet. The old cemetery on the hill contains tombstones of many young people (often dying of illness or accident in the early years) and a sailor killed in the skirmish with the Kake.

James Swan outside his office with
Rothschild House above, ca. 1885
UW Libraries, Special Collections,
UW3840

Post Office / James Swan's Office: Lucy's father is fictional. But a great description of Judge Swan and his office from the *Register* influenced scenes of Lucy visiting her father at work.

Description of Swan's office; his office mate giving candy to a child
Port Townsend Register, April 4, 1860: UW Libraries, Special Collections, 18600404

Law and Justice.

Major VanBokkelen the United States Commissioner and Mr. Swan the Justice of the Peace, and committing Magistrate, have their offices in the back room of the Post Office building, where the Major also officiates as Post master. The front room is a sort of news room and place for loungers to wile away their time over newspapers. Here the Major can be found at all times, ready in his brusque off hand manner and loud voice, to pass his opinion on law points, attend to the postal affairs of the United States, or sell a penny whistle to a child. The Commissioner and the Magistrate are both pretty off hand in their decisions, and the wheels of justice are never delayed on their account.

Rothschild and The Kentucky Store (Mrs. Blanc):   Mrs. Blanc is fictional, but her house is real. David C. H. Rothschild moved to Port Townsend in 1858 and built The Kentucky Store. In 1868 he built his home, quite fancy for the time. The family was active and social, and known for having many pets. Rothschild's daughter Emilie grew up there and stayed until her death in 1954, leaving the house almost unchanged. It did have a stream through the basement and a water pump in the kitchen, a very modern item!

Rothschild House today, with Whidbey Island in the distance
A. Davey, under Creative Commons license 2.0

Ad for The Kentucky Store and Rothschild
Port Townsend Register, January 18, 1860; UW Libraries, Special Collections, 1860018 002

Sooke: súʔəkʷ

Vancouver Island / The House with Stars in the Roof: A long-house on Vancouver Island did have holes cut in the roof to imi-tate the night sky. The S'Klallam are closely related to the Sooke on Vancouver Island. This detail and the folk tale about the maid-ens who married stars are taken from Erna Gunther's works. (*See Bibliography.*)

People

William Bishop, Founder of Chimacum:

Senator William Bishop, Jr. in an auto, Port Townsend
UW Libraries, Special Collections, UW5095

Chimacum area: čə́məqʼəm

As a sailor in the English navy, Bishop's life was harsh. He jumped ship in Victoria and made his way to Port Townsend, finding work as a hired hand. He built up a large dairy farm in Chimacum. His son would have still been a baby in 1862, so Matthias is fictional.

Ledgers for Bishop's farm sold with this introduction: "He established a… dairy business and sold his produce in Port Townsend, making the day-long trip by horse and wagon. In 1877… he had sold 6,881 pounds of butter." http://www.msrarebooks. com/4DCGI/w_BookDetailS/24441

William Bishop, Junior (the real son), served in the Washington State Senate for many years. His mother Sally was from the Snohomish tribe, and they did have two parlors in a fine house. He bought another farm in the valley, and his family still runs a dairy there today.

The Brinnons: Elwell P. Brinnon founded Brinnon on Hood Canal. He married Chetzmoka's sister and they had a son, but later than the time of the story. So, William is fictional.

**Chief Chetzemoka
(Chee-mah-hum or T'Chits-a-mahun):**
Chetzmoka, chief of the S'Klallam tribe, was about 40 when the first settlers arrived in 1851. In the 1850s he was taken to San Francisco and shown the power of the American military. Settlers called him *Duke of York* and his son *Prince of Wales*. His brother was said to be quarrelsome, but there is no mention of him running alcohol. A statue in Port Townsend honors Chetzemoka for helping to keep the peace at a tense time; the town also named a park for him. The 274-foot-long ferry *Chetzemoka* launched in 2010, but serves on a different route.

Image courtesy
Elaine Grinnell and the
Jamestown S'Klallam tribe

Elaine Grinnell (Quill): Quill is fictional, but the name is from **Kwəlcid**, the S'Klallam name of Elaine Grinnell. Elaine is story-keeper and elder for the Jamestown S'Klallam Tribe. She heard many of her stories from her grandfather, David Prince, while they sat by the stove and waited for black-outs to end during WWII. Prince learned them from *his* grandfather, *Chetzemoka*.

great-great-grandparent/child: háʔkʷiyaʔqʷ

In December of 2015, I was blessed to hear Elaine in Blyn. She brought the stories to life with such charm and spirit. Many of them reminded me of Irish folk tales, and she remarked that cultures near water often share similar stories. She also told stories about her grandfather, like driving the tractor for him when she was very young because he had terrible arthritis.

Isaac Ebey, Founder of Whidbey Island: Isaac N. Ebey staked the first claim on Whidbey Island in 1850, under the *Donation Land Claim Act*. His green valley dips down to the water opposite Port Townsend and is rich farmland. Isaac convinced his family to travel out as he had—by way of the Oregon Trail. (See letters following.)

Mrs. Blanc is fictional, but accounts of Ebey's death are true, as related by his brother Winfield.

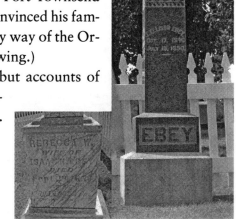

Sunnyside Cemetery overlooks the Ebey Reserve. Isaac and his wife are buried there, along with his parents, and other family members. A number of them died young, of tuberculosis.

James G. Swan: James Swan, early settler and collector for the Smithsonian, served as a judge and wrote a well-known book about the Makah. He met Chetzemoka in San Francisco and the chief convinced him to move to Port Townsend. The two became close friends, and Swan did save the life of the chief's infant son—Prince of Wales, Elaine's great grandfather.

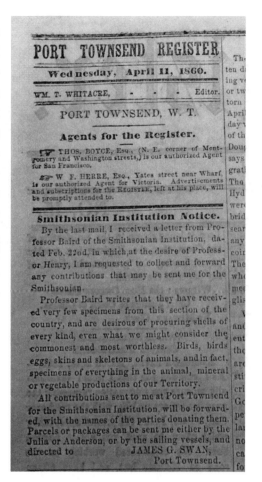

James Swan asks for items to send to the Smithsonian
Port Townsend Register, April 11, 1860;
UW Libraries, Special Collections,
18600411

Events

Gold!: Gold was found along the Fraser River in the mid 1800s. Port Townsend happily sold goods to miners and sailors on their way north—everything from ships' anchors to candles.

The Incident that Led to the Scalping: In 1856, a group of Tlingit from Kake, Alaska camped outside the Port Gamble Mill. The workers inside called in the military. When the Kake refused to

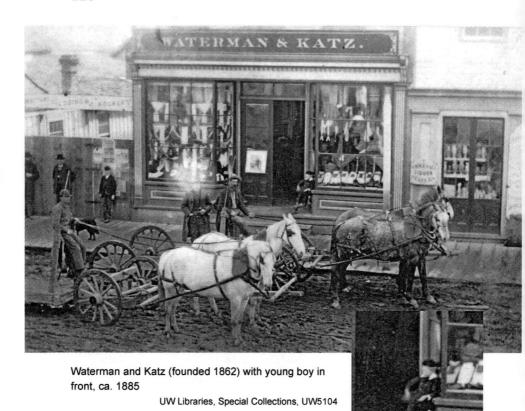

Waterman and Katz (founded 1862) with young boy in front, ca. 1885

leave, the *USS Massachusetts* opened fire. Twenty-seven members of the tribe were killed, including women and a chief. The Kake sent a war party a year later, wanting revenge—a chief for a chief, according to their culture. The man they wanted was away, so they chose Isaac Ebey (a leader, but not involved in the incident). On August 11, 1857, Ebey was shot and scalped. His wife and children escaped out a window and hid in the trees. His brother found Ebey's body.

Kake Visit Site of Ebey's Death 157 Years Later: Members of the Kake tribe visited Whidbey in 2014. Kake elders and local historians talked about the incident and the loss of life on both sides. The article by Ron Newberry from August 20, 2014 can be found in the archives of the Whidbey News Times.

Swan Saves Prince of Wales: A smallpox plague struck hard in 1859. Chetzemoka's ten-month-old baby fell gravely ill. He thought his son had died and laid him outside, as the family was too sick to bury him. Two days later, Swan "came to the village to see how his stricken friends were faring. Passing the smokehouse, he was startled to hear a feeble whimper from within."* Swan rescued the baby, who later became the father of David Prince. (*Mary Ann Lambert in *Shadows of Our Ancestors,* who said, "The hardest hit was the house of Chet-ze-moka...Lach-ka-num.")

Looking down at the harbor from the steps, Port Townsend, ca. 1885
University of Washington Libraries, Special Collections UW3841

S'klallam Branches and Traditions

Clallam, Klallam, S'Klallam, Indian, First Nation:
Klallam: nəxʷsƛ́áy̓əm̓

S'Klallam means *Strong People*. Settlers used *Clallam* for the tribe, a bay, and a county. The tribe uses *S'Klallam*, but *Klallam* also appears often. All three appear in *Cradle*. At the time period of the book, *Indian* was used (and still seems to be in Washington State). In British Columbia, *First Nations* is used to describe first settlers in the area. A member of the Jamestown S'Klallam told me they prefer to be called by the name of their particular tribe: hence *Klallam or S'Klallam*.

Quiver courtesy Elaine Grinnell

Baskets and Hats / Weaving: Weaving is a beloved and honored art. S'Klallam weavers harvest cedar from particular trees each year to make their strong—even watertight—baskets. Strength is required to grab a strip of bark and yank upwards to detach it, but never so much as to harm the tree. In the book the girls weave in the wrong season, so they soak the cedar to soften it. Cedar hats were important for the wet weather, and still appear on rainy days!

Hat courtesy Elaine Grinnell

make a basket:
čáy ʔaʔ či muhúy̓

Blankets from Rare Dogs: Northwest tribes bred white dogs and used their fur mixed with goose down for blankets. These disappeared quickly when the striped Hudson's Bay blankets arrived. If one of the white blankets existed in the time of the story, it would have been valuable and rare.

any blanket: sémiʔ; łqít

Games: Gambling with bones and stones, rolling hoops, and foot races were popular.

slahal, stick game, bone game: sləhál

Naming: Families took time to see a child's personality before giving a final name. Troublesome children sometimes didn't receive a name for many years!

Mixed Marriages: Many settlers married Indian women, often of great status and beauty (like Brinnon and Chetzemoka's sister). William Bishop's marriage to Sally (Klasistook) ended in divorce, but Sally's descendants still farm the land her son William bought in Chimacum.

A sad story relates to the lovely Seam-Itza, a S'Klallam princess. She married a settler for love, but hung herself after her husband's sister visited unexpectedly. He hadn't told his family that his beautiful wife also happened to be an Indian. Seam-Itza left her house in perfect order, with two pies freshly baked. No one knows what the sister said, but suicide may have been the young wife's way of protesting an insult. (related by Mary Ann Lambert in *Shadows of our Ancestors*)

Songs and Lullabies: For the S'Klallam, land wasn't thought of as something to be owned; but a person did own their songs and dances. When women married, they brought their songs with them, and this was a form of wealth.

sing a song: ťíyəm

lullaby: sťíym

Two U.S. tribes are famous for their lullabies—the Pueblo and the Makah. Traditional Makah and Klallam areas overlap, so the skill might have been shared. Quill's father is fictional, but he's the type of man who would sing to his little ones. "The men of the tribe were very fond of the children, and there were special songs that men sang to the children at home. A man would take the baby, 'dance it,' and sing." (Frances Densmore, in *Weave Little Stars into My Sleep*.)

Jamestown, Port Gamble, and Lower Elwha S'Klallam

Jamestown: The S'Klallam originally lived along the straits between roughly Port Angeles and the mouth of Puget Sound. After the 1855 treaty, families were forced out of their traditional areas, and some families settled in Jamestown (near Sequim). After many quiet years, the Jamestown S'Klallam secured federal recognition and funding, and built a tribal center in Blyn.

Jamestown: stətíłəm; ċicə́qʷ; čšcə́qʷ

Lower Elwha Tribe, River and Dam: The Lower Elwha Klallam have been involved with a big project in Washington: the removal of a dam on the Elwha River. Salmon—a key part of Klallam culture—had almost died out on the river. In early 2016, as part of restoring the ecosystem, the river was shifted back into its original channel for the first time in 100 years. The project can easily be found online.

Elwha River: ʔéʔɬxʷaʔ

For the Port Gamble S'Klallam, see entry on Port Gamble.

Excerpts from Original Journals, Newspapers, Letters

James G. Swan Journals

Swan kept track of everything in his journals and many details for *Cradle* were found there, written in his beautiful script. Particularly helpful were: fishing trips, weather, mail, shipping details, remedies for wounds, and political news. He was reading *Les Miserables*, though it had just been published a year before in Paris (in 1862)! This reveals that the town, which got many current items by ship, lived very differently than inland pioneers.

"Morning delightful, calm and warm. After breakfast... started for Chimacum Creek with the Duke of York and Jimmy Lind and accompanied by General Gaines, Queen Victoria and Mrs. Gaines, Queen Victoria's little boy and a little girl. We passed several canoes containing Indians fishing, all of whom paid a tribute to the Duke by presents of fish... Stopped at Chimacum Point to get clams. Found plenty of trout at 7 the mills and had a grand feast of fish."

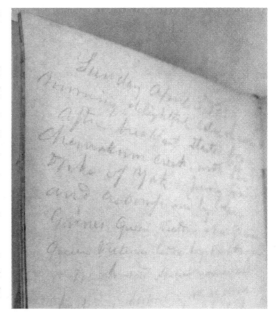

Fishing with the Chief, April 3, 1859: Swan's 1859 journal, open to an entry about fishing with Chetzemoka: Swan refers to him as *Duke of York* and his wives as *Queen Victoria and Jenny Lind (misspelled as Jimmy in archives).*
UW Libraries, Special Collections, PNW00672. Image by author

Dreadful News, April 20, 1865:

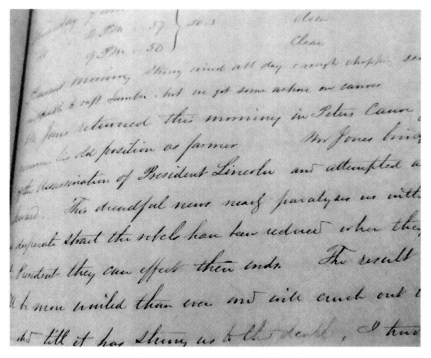

Swan's entry the day he hears of Lincoln's assassination, shortly after an entry about the war ending.

"Mr. Jones brings the sad intelligence of the assassination of President Lincoln and attempted assassination of Secretary Seward. This dreadful news nearly paralyses us with grief and shows to what desperate strait the rebels have been reduced when they can think that by killing the President they can effect their ends."

Isaac Ebey Letters

Ebey moved out first and was later joined by his wife and parents. His tender letters home include important events in the early years of the Territory, and creative spelling!

Pacific Ocean.
Brig. Orbit Feb. 20th 1850.
My Dear Parents,

I once more set myself down to write you from this quarter of the world. I have wrote home so often with out being favored with a single line from those who are dearer to me than life its self. I am almost persuaded to believe I am forgotten or only remembered as one who once was.

Our cargo consists of 35.000 feet of plank, 400.000 cedar shingles, Irish potatoes, Butter, cheeses & etc. We pay $75 per Thousand for Lumber, $10 per Thousand for singles, three Dollars per bushel for potatoes, Beets, Carrots & 10 cents per pound for Butter, 40 cts for Cheese. ...A man can now make more money in Oregon than he can in California unless he is in some verry profitable business.

A great deal of improvement will be done this summer on the Sound. Mills will go up, towns located, merchants flocking into the Country and all things going ahead. The sound is bound to be the Second place on the Pacific Ocean. San Francisco will always be first. The vast amount of timber that will be consumed in California and the Sandwich Islands all of which have to come from Oregon make this a very desirable location for those who want to make money and enjoy good health.

Letter to Isacc's wife, Rebecca (June 8, 1851):
UW Libraries, Special Collections, PNW00402; all images by author.

My Dear Rebecca,

Your esteemed favor of 17th. Feb. came to hand yesterday. Your letters always fall on my heart like a shower of rain on the thirsty earth, it refreshes and vivifies my whole nature. In your letter you make some wise and excellent suggestions; I shall act upon them, and thank you for them. I am satisfied that a man can never take better counsels then from his wife, his bosom companion. If any thing reconciles me to another years separation, it is that you, aunt Martha, and Father's people will all come together. ...Rebecca my love, I write this letter with a better heart and pleasanter feeling that I have written many a long day; take good care of your health. I will not say to you watch over the little boys, that you will do anyhow.

* * *

Oh how I desier to be with my children to watch the opening of there youthful minds. I want them to be inteligent and would like to see them far than advanced in there Books than any other children of their age. ...I would like you, if you can get these, to bring out some onions seed that the first year produces setes, then transplanted the second year; onion seed in this country is very scarce. ... Now Rebecca it is fit that I should bring this long letter to a close, word used upon paper is but a poor substitute for the language of the heart, such at least as my heart feels and yearns towards you, would that that I could writer better , but in the absence of such you must be content with this as a substitute. The little locks of hare came safe. I look at them every day and kiss them.

I am very bussy now a working at my crop, my wheat is just begginning to head. this letter is the works of odd hours for several days. Remember me affectionately to your Dear Mother and Thomas and Sister Martha, to Uncle Samuel, Aunt Polly and Martha and all the children, I expect Margarete is nearly grown. kiss her for me and tell her I think of her very, very often and would be glad to get a line from her in a corner of your letters at any time.

Visit my people as often as convenient and try and cheer up the feeling of my Dear old mother. Write to me after and believe you write so as to do [illegible] of your starting, I shall be here to meet you at Fort Hall or East of there.

Farewell Rebecca for the present I hope this time next you will find us approaching each other in different directions. from yours ever a faithful husband,

I N. Ebey

Port Townsend Register Excerpts

The *Register* was the first newspaper in town, founded in 1859. Swan describes a cannon being fired to celebrate the event. Many events in *Cradle* were taken from stories in the *Register*.

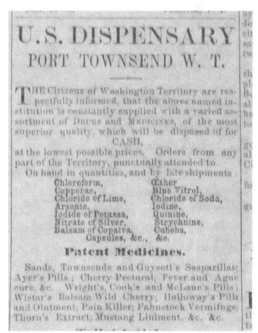

Ad for medicine and toilet articles
Port Townsend Register, January 18, 1860; UW Libraries, Special Collections, 1860018

Col. Ebey's Scalp.

A. M. Poe, Esq., who arrived here from Victoria a few days since, showed us the scalp of the late lamented Col. Isaac N. Ebey, the former Collector of the Puget Sound District. Col. Ebey at the time he was massacred, was residing at his house on Whidby's Island near Ebey's landing. A party of Kake Indians, a tribe residing 750 miles north of Victoria, had called at his house the day previous, and had been kindly received. The following night they came, and after calling Col. Ebey out of his house, they shot him, then cut off his head and made good their escape. This murder was on the night of the 11th of August, 1857. Since that time repeated endeavors have been made to recover the head but without effect, until sometime last fall, Capt. Dodd of the H. B. Co's steamer Labouchere managed to procure the scalp, which he brought to Victoria and presented to Mr. Poe, to be given by him to the relations of Col. Ebey.

The scalp was cut from the forehead entirely around the skull, to the roots of the hair on the back of the neck, and includes one half of both ears. The beautiful brown hair, fine and silky in its appearance, is as natural as when in life it covered the head of the brave, worthy man.—Many of the intimate friends of the late Colonel recognized the sad relics, and with it came crowding back the remembrance of those dark and bloody days, from the horrors of which, our

Port Townsend Register, April 11, 1860; UW Libraries, Special Collections, 18600411

Swan and Chetzemoka intervene for escaped slave; British government supports 'husband'.

Port Townsend Register, March 28, 1860; UW Libraries, Special Collections, 18600328.001

Fugitive Slaves.

The following correspondence relative to the slave which *old Yank* rescued from bondage— an account of which can be found on our first page—has taken place between the authorities of Vancouver's Island, and "one of the Magistrates of Washington Territory." After all the tattle of the British about no slavery existing on British soil, it does look a little remarkable that Gov. Douglas should set himself up as a slave catcher for fugitives from Indian bondage. If the slave alluded to had been black, with curly hair, British sympathies would have been loud to have had her returned to her parents. But, LO! the poor Indian is red, and fashionable emancipators have not yet come up to that standard of color:

VICTORIA, Vancouver's Island,
20th March, 1860.

[Seal.] *To the Magistrate or Magistrates of Washington Territory:*

SIR:—I am directed by His Excellency, the Governor of Vancouver's Island, to state that the bearer of this note is a native of Victoria, Vancouver's Island, and a person of quiet deportment, and good character. He is about to proceed to Port Townsend in search of a wife or daughter, who has either fled or been forcibly abducted from this place, and his case is hereby recommended for the consideration of the Magistrates of Washington Territory; and in order that they may kindly assist him in the recovery of the object he is search of. I have the honor to be,

Your most ob't. sv't.,
PHILIP M. NAID.

The above was sent to Port Townsend by an Indian of the Songish tribe of Victoria, the owner of the slave. The following was the reply of the Magistrate, which was sent by the Indian on his return:

PORT TOWNSEND, March 26, 1860.

The fugitive alluded to in the foregoing, is an Indian girl, who was held as a slave by the bearer of this note—an Indian of the Songish tribe. It appears upon examination, that the girl is a Chemakum Indian, and that her parents are now living in this town. There is no law between the United States and Great Britain relative to the rendition of fugitive slaves, and Magistrates have no authority in this Territory to exercise a jurisdiction in the case.

Very respectfully, your most ob't.,
JAMES G. SWAN,
Justice of the Peace.

To PHILIP M. NAID, ESQ.,
Victoria, V. I.

The case was referred to the "Duke of York," who stated that he would "mamoke tumtum," which he did, by deciding that the father of the slave girl must pay the Songish Indian ten blankets, and if that did not satisfy him for the price of the girl, he might return to Victoria with such fleas in his ear as he had caught during his mission to Port Townsend.

Chetzemoka and Swan, Slaves and Raids:

Northern tribes like the Haida and Tlingit had guns before other tribes and made regular raids, traveling as much as 1,000 miles in huge canoes. Local tribes had similar clashes. William Bishop described a raiding party in 1857 that massacred most of the Chimakum in retribution for their frequent attacks on neighbors. An interesting issue with a woman taken to Victoria, who escaped and returned home to Chimacum. Both Chetzemoka and Swan weighed in.

Offensive piece about Indians in Port Townsend, wishing they'd leave the land
Port Townsend Register,
March 28, 1860;
UW Libraries, Special
Collections, 18600328.002

REMOVAL OF THE INDIANS FROM THE CITY LIMITS.—We understand that a proposition will be submitted to the next meeting of the City Trustees, to have the Indians now living here, removed beyond the limits of the city. This is a movement very much needed, for the space occupied by the lodges of the Clallams at the upper part of the town, and of the Chemakums at Point Hudson, covers much valuable property that is needed for building purposes. Besides the unsightly appearance of the smoky, filthy huts of the savages, the appearance of the half-naked, unwashed, uncombed, and greasy occupants, who wander about our streets, exhibiting themselves in a manner offensive to the eyes of decency, is a matter that the city government will do well to attend to, and have the nuisance abated. But we do not think it right or just to be too precipitate in the matter, nor would we wish to put the Indians to unnecessary trouble and expense. It is probable that the next mail may bring us the intelligence that Congress has passed the appropriation necessary for carrying into effect the Indian Treaties. If so, but a few weeks at the farthest, can elapse, before they will be placed on their Reservations; and having so long put up with the nuisance, we can afford to abide by it for a few weeks longer, without any serious detriment to our interests.

Interview with Elaine Grinnell
A Time of Sorrow at Kahtai

Washington State Historical Society hosts an Elaine Grinnell page with links to S'Klallam baskets and items, and also a transcript of an interview. She gives poignant details about the fire at Kahtai, events which involved her grandfather's grandfather (Chetzemoka).

"I would say that most of my stories came from my experiences with my grandmother and grandfather. I was raised by them. And Klallam was their first language.

They liked where the Klallams were living in Port Townsend. That's what you now know as Kahtai. In fact that's what we called Port Townsend, Kahtai. There were Klallam there, all the fishing was there, fresh water was there. The deer were there, crabs, salmon... right there.

A natural harbor also. They could have their canoes any place they wanted to down there. But it was also a good place for ships. And pretty soon they were treated so badly that it was very difficult to live there. And then the chief realized that there were more Klallams in the cemetery than there were in the village. And about that same time it was decided by the government that the Klallams should be down on the reservation, down at Skokomish..."
(Chief and families decide to return to Port Townsend instead of going to Skokomish in canoes.)

"But when they got there they found that their houses were burning. It's hard for us to put words to a feeling like that... to see your home burning. There's such a finality to it. It's very close to death.... Treatment got very bizarre after that. So they knew that they had to move on. Some went to Port Gamble. Luckily some stayed back... the Lower Elwhas were on the west end anyway. But they had the same kind of experience."

For the full interview and photos of S'Klallam artifacts see: www.washingtonhistory.org/research/whc/WHCcollections/ localgrants/nhroralhistory/Grinnell/

SELECT BIBLIOGRAPHY

Cooper, James and G. Suckley. *The Natural History of Washington Territory with Much Relating to Minnesota, Nebraska, Kansas, Oregon, and California.* New York: Baillière Brothers, 1859.

Gorsline, Jerry, ed. *Shadows of Our Ancestors: Readings in the History of Klallam-White Relations.* Port Townsend: Empty Bowl, 1992. (Source for story of young farm wife.)

Gunther, Erna. *Klallam Ethnography* and *Klallam Folk Tales.* Seattle: University of Washington Press, 1927. (Rich source for details, including: *Star Husband* story, hoop game, first weir for salmon, salmon drying, wool from dogs, longhouse with stars in the roof.)

Hamm, Diane Johnston. *Daughter of Suqua.* Morton Grove: Albert Whitman & Co., 1997. (Young Suquamish girl sent away to residential school and local school shut.)

Hermanson, James S. *Port Townsend Memories.* Port Townsend: Hermanson, 2001. (Essays originally in *The Port Townsend Leader*, based on interviews with early families.)

McGuffey's Second Eclectic Reader. New York: Van Antwerp, Bragg & Co., 1879.

Philip, Neil. *Weave Little Stars into My Sleep: Native American Lullabies.* New York: Clarion, 2001. (Makah lullabies, woman harvesting shellfish in a cedar hat while standing in tide pool.)

Simpson, Peter, ed. *City of Dreams: A Guide to Port Townsend.* Port Townsend: Bay Press, 1986.

James G. Swan Journals. University of Washington. (Digital and physical versions: see excerpts.)

Key Websites

Bishop farm ledgers, M & S Rare Books, accessed October, 2015 (w/ excellent Bishop history).

Gerald Bishop (Bishop Dairy Farm), Organic Valley, accessed December, 2015.

David Prince, Olympic Peninsula Pioneer Obituaries, Peninsula Daily News.

Interview with Elaine Grinnell, Washington State Historical Society.

Jefferson County Historical Timeline: 1592-2007, Jefferson County Historical Society.

*Klallam Wordlist. (*Source of all Klallam words in the book, except "limpet" from Gunther's *Klallam Ethnography*).

Timeline, Elwha Klallam Tribe.

ACKNOWLEDGEMENTS

This book would still be an awkward draft without the friends who've read along in all its stages. I think of them as friends of the book as well, and I'm so grateful for each one. A stellar friend of the book is Susan Zwinger, author of fine natural history books and teacher of artful journaling. Thanks to Susan for offering support and enthusiasm at a critical moment, and for the lovely blurb.

Librarians can be magical creatures. Those at the University of Washington Special Collections helped at every stage, especially with finding and photographing rare materials. A volunteer at the Jacob Ebey House shared choice facts with me, and still farms the land Isaac Ebey claimed. Local history heroes at the Jefferson Historical Society provided clues in the early stages of my research and access to Rothschild House on a cold winter day. I wouldn't know about the creek in the basement without them!

The Jamestown S'Klallam tribe has been so welcoming. Elder and historian Kathy Duncan kindly read the whole book, and it is much richer for her input. I'm particularly indebted to her for details about basket weaving, harvesting cedar, potlatch, naming, songs and what is and isn't property.

Many thanks to Elaine Grinnell for sharing with me about her family's life and James Swan's friendship with Chetzemoka, and for giving me her S'Klallam name to use. She is a master storyteller and it was a delight to hear her in December of 2015. Thanks to John Adams, a schoolmate from Sequim, who put me in touch with his amazing neighbor.

Nina Noble has done an outstanding job on design, cover art, and maps for the book, and is a fabulous human. Edward Bolme lent his keen eye to proofing and editing while pursuing a few other things, like his day job. I'm so grateful for his time, talents and friendship!

Gratitude to the friendly and helpful Brendan Clark at Village Books Publishing in Bellingham. For an outstanding bookstore, farmer's market, local coffee and brews, Bellingham fits the bill. (Plus a dog park that Chester loves.) It's a wag-worthy place.

No words could fully express thanks to my family, but I made an attempt...at the front.

It truly takes a village to raise any child, including one made of paper and ink.

Love to my village,

Anne-Marie Heckt
Edmonds, Washington
May 2016

AFTERWORD

We moved to a town near Port Townsend when I was young. It was difficult being from the outside, so my story is a little like Lucy's. I went to school with S'Klallam families, but I didn't know much about the tribe at the time. I've enjoyed getting to know more about this Strong People.

I have also enjoyed the stories of those who looked for a new life in Port Townsend, often fleeing poverty or hardship. Their courage and energy are amazing to read about, and some of their descendants still farm there. It's worth a visit to enjoy the forests and beaches, but also to follow in the footsteps of a pioneer generation. Their fingerprints appear everywhere, as soon as you begin to look for them.

In 1862 we were a nation torn by the Civil War. Now we are a nation torn by economic inequality, political, religious and racial strife. Perhaps by stepping into the shoes of those living in a different time, we can learn to better hear the voices of others.

May we honor all who have gone before us and formed these places, and be mindful of those who will walk here after us... and of the land and waters which sustain us all.

CPSIA information can be obtained
at www.ICGtesting.com
Printed in the USA
FSOW01n0632270616
22035FS